Marian's Favorite Bible Stories

by

MARIAN M. SCHOOLLAND

Illustrations in Full Color by
DIRK GRINGHUIS

WM. B. EERDMANS PUBLISHING COMPANY
Grand Rapids, Michigan

THE PICTURES

Adam petted the animals, one by one, and gave each one a name 10

God told Noah he could leave the ark. What a happy day that was! 19

At the well, Jacob met Rachel and helped water the sheep 30

How glad Jacob was to see his son Joseph again! 39

By night God led them with the Pillar of Fire 50

Samson grew up to be very strong; one day he killed a lion 59

Elijah said, "The God who sends fire, he will be the true God." 70

The angel said to the shepherds, "Do not be afraid!" 79

Nicodemus came at night, to talk with Jesus alone 90

Jesus taught the people lessons from the lilies and the birds 99

Mary ran to tell the disciples, "I have seen Jesus. He is alive!" 110

A light brighter than the sun blinded Saul, and he was afraid 119

THE STORIES

1. How the World Began   7
2. The First People   8
3. God's Beautiful Earth Is Spoiled   12
4. The Children of Adam and Eve   13
5. A Great Flood   15
6. The Rainbow   17
7. A Friend of God   21
8. Abraham and Isaac   23
9. God Answers Prayer   25
10. Jacob and Esau   26
11. Jacob Finds a New Home   28
12. Joseph, the Dreamer   32
13. Joseph in Prison   34
14. Joseph in the Palace   35
15. Joseph's Brothers   37
16. Joseph and Jacob Meet Again   38
17. A Baby in a Basket   42
18. The Burning Bush   44
19. Pharaoh Says "No" to God   46
20. God Sets His People Free   47
21. A Path Through the Sea   51
22. The Shining Serpent   52
23. The Walls of Jericho   53
24. Brave Gideon   55
25. Ruth Chooses for God   56
26. Samson, the Strong Man   58
27. Samuel, the Temple Boy   62
28. David, the Shepherd Boy   63
29. David and the Giant   64
30. David Runs Away   65

31. David Becomes King   67
32. Fire from Heaven   71
33. A Widow's Oil   73
34. A Letter for God to Read   74
35. A Book That Told the Truth   75
36. Daniel in the Lions' Den   77
37. God Sends His Son   78
38. God Makes Two Old People Happy   82
39. Jesus' Star   83
40. Jesus in His Father's House   84
41. A Voice From Heaven   86
42. Two Men Visit Jesus   87
43. Jesus Calls His Disciples   88
44. A Visit at Night   91
45. Four Fishermen   92
46. Down Through the Roof   94
47. Jesus Turns Tears to Smiles   96
48. A Foolish Rich Man   97
49. A Lesson From Lilies and Birds   98
50. Jesus Raises a Little Girl   101
51. A Little Boy's Lunch Grows Big   103
52. Jesus Walks on the Waves   105
53. Three Crosses on a Hill   106
54. The Resurrection   108
55. Two Men Walk With Jesus   112
56. Jesus Comes Through a Closed Door   113
57. Jesus Comes to the Disciples Again   114
58. A Meeting by the Lake   115
59. The Man by the Temple Gate   117
60. Jesus Calls Saul   118
61. An Earthquake Opens Prison   122
62. A Shipwreck   123
63. John's Vision   124

1

How the World Began

(*Genesis 1*)

Long, long ago, there were no people in the world. There was not even a world. There was no sun in the sky; there was no moon; there were no stars. In all the wide, wide space there was nothing. There was only God. God was everywhere.

Then God made the earth, the great big ball on which we live.

At first the earth was all dark, as darkest night. But God said, "Let there be light!" and there was light! That was the first morning of the first day.

After a while the light slipped away. Night came. But after the night, morning came again. That was the second day.

On the second day, the earth was all watery with mist. God sent some of the water up into the sky, to be clouds. Some of it stayed below, and covered the earth.

On the third day, God spoke to the water on the earth. He told it to come together in great oceans, so that the land would be dry. Then God spoke again, and plants came up on the dry land. Grass grew, and trees and bushes and flowers. When night came the earth was pretty with green plants and blue oceans.

Once again morning came. That was the fourth day. On this day God set the great lights in the sky. He made the sun to shine by day. He made the moon and stars to shine at night.

Then came the fifth day. The sun arose in the east. It shone on the green grass and on the trees and flowers. It shone on the blue oceans. Everything was bright and pretty in the sunshine.

But the earth was very quiet. There was not one bird to sing in the trees. There was not one fish to play in the water.

Then God gave command for birds and fish to be. And there they were! Birds flew in the air. Fishes swam in the water. The birds sang praises to God. The big and little fishes played and splashed.

On the sixth day God made the animals. He made little furry ones, and big long-legged ones, some with long necks, and some with long tails. He made all kinds of animals to play in the green grass and climb up the trees.

That is how the world began. And when God looked at all the things He had made, He saw that the earth was very beautiful and very good.

2

The First People

(Genesis 2)

God made the earth, with all the plants and animals. And then He made man.

God made this man from the earth. He made a body with arms and legs; He made a head, with wonderful eyes and ears and nose and mouth. Then God breathed into the man and he was alive. He stood up before God, a fine, big, strong man.

God called the man Adam. And God made a beautiful garden where Adam could live. In the garden there were flowers, and there were trees with wonderful fruit. It was the Garden of Eden. God told Adam to take care of the beautiful garden and live there.

One day God brought all the animals to Adam—a whole long row of them. God told Adam to give names to all the animals.

Adam loved the animals. He was not afraid of them, and they were not afraid of him. Adam petted them, one by one, and he gave each one a name. The little furry chipmunk, the rabbit with long ears, the big elephant, the frisky squirrel, the woolly sheep—Adam named them all. There were tiny animals, too—the busy ant, the buzzing bee, and the pretty butterfly. When Adam had named them all, they all ran off to work and play again.

But Adam was lonesome. The animals could play together. Adam had no one to talk to and live with.

God knew Adam was lonesome. So one day God put Adam to sleep. While Adam was asleep, God took a rib from his side, and God made a beautiful woman.

After a while Adam awoke. Then God brought the beautiful woman to him. When Adam saw her, he was very glad. He loved her. And he called her Eve.

Adam and Eve took care of the garden. They ate the good fruit, and listened to the birds, and smelled the perfume of the pretty flowers. Sometimes God came down from heaven to talk with them. Adam and Eve were very happy.

Adam petted the animals, one
by one, and gave each one a name.

3

God's Beautiful Earth Is Spoiled

(*Genesis 2, 3*)

Our earth was once a lovely place. There was nothing bad or ugly anywhere on it. There were no thorns to prick your fingers. The bees would not sting you and the lions would not roar at you.

At that time there were only two people upon the earth—just Adam and Eve. They lived in the beautiful garden. God had given them the garden, with all its flowers and fruit.

God said to them, "You may eat the fruit of the garden. You may eat of all the trees except one. The tree in the middle of the garden is the Tree of Knowledge of Good and Evil. You may not eat the fruit of that tree. If you do eat it, you will surely die."

But one day, when Eve was walking in the garden, a serpent talked to her. It was not really the serpent who talked. It was Satan, hiding inside the serpent. Satan is an evil spirit who hates God.

Satan said to Eve, "Did God tell you not to eat of the fruit of the garden?"

Eve said, "Oh no! We may eat fruit from all the trees except one. We may not eat the fruit of the Tree of Knowledge of Good and Evil. That is the tree in the middle of the garden. If we do, God says we will die."

Then Satan said, "No, you will not die if you eat that fruit. Instead, it will make you wise like God!"

Then Eve went to look at that tree. It was pretty, and the fruit looked good to eat. Eve reached up and picked it. And then she ate it.

After that she called Adam, and he ate some of it, too.

So Adam and Eve disobeyed God.

In the evening, when God came to talk with Adam and Eve, they were afraid. They tried to hide from God.

But nobody can hide from God.

God called Adam. And Adam had to come out of his hiding place.

God said to Adam and Eve, "Because you disobeyed me, thorns and weeds shall grow on the earth. You shall have to work hard. You shall have much pain and sorrow. And at last you shall die."

Then God sent them out of the beautiful garden.

That is how our beautiful earth was spoiled. That is why we have pain and sorrow now. That is why God does not come down to earth to walk and talk with us now.

But God did make a way for us to go to Him. He sent Jesus Christ to be our Saviour. We can go to God by praying to Him in Jesus' name.

4

The Children of Adam and Eve

(Genesis 4)

God still loved Adam and Eve. He still watched over them. He let them pray to Him. He showed them how to make an altar of stones.

They were to burn their best animals on the altar, as an offering to God for sin. God heard their prayers, when they said they were sorry for their sins.

After a while God gave children to Adam and Eve. The first baby was a boy. Adam and Eve were very happy to have a baby. They called him Cain. The next baby was a boy, too. They called him Abel. Then there were many other children, boys and girls.

When Cain grew up, he made a garden. He had fruits and vegetables. Abel became a shepherd. He had many sheep and lambs.

One day Cain and Abel were in the field together.

Cain said to himself, "Today I shall bring a gift to God on my altar."

So Cain took some of the grain and fruit of his garden. He laid them on the altar and burned them to God.

But Cain did not love God. As he watched the gift burn on the altar, Cain was not happy. He knew, deep down in his heart, that God did not want his gift. God wants us to love Him first. Then He will take our gifts.

Cain looked up. He saw Abel. Abel, too, was bringing a gift to God. Abel had taken a lamb from his flock. He was offering it on his altar to God. Cain watched him. He saw Abel lay the lamb on the altar and burn it. He saw that Abel's face was happy.

The lamb on the altar was a picture of Jesus dying for our sins.

But Cain said, "God takes Abel's gift. He does not want mine." And Cain was angry.

Then Cain heard a voice call to him. It was God's voice. God said, "Cain, why are you angry? If you do well, you will be accepted; if not, sin is at the door of your heart."

But Cain did not care. He was very angry. He doubled his fist and went to Abel. He talked to Abel. Anger filled his heart more and more. At last he hit Abel. Cain hit Abel so hard that Abel fell down dead.

Cain saw Abel fall. But he turned and went away.

Then God's voice called Cain again. God asked, "Cain, where is your brother Abel?"

Cain did not dare to say what he had done. He answered, "Must I take care of my brother?"

But God knew what Cain had done. God knows everything.

God said to Cain, "Because you have done this great sin, your garden will never grow for you again. You shall wander around, far from home. You must find your food here and there. You shall be a wanderer."

Then Cain was afraid.

Cain said, "What shall become of me? If I go and wander up and down, somebody will find me and kill me."

But God had mercy on Cain. God said, "I will not let anyone kill you." And He put a mark on Cain, so that no one would kill him.

So Cain left his home. He took his wife along. They wandered away to a far country.

Adam and Eve were very sorry to lose two of their boys. Now they knew that their sin had come upon their children.

5

A Great Flood

(Genesis 6, 7)

Once upon a time, many years ago, God looked down upon the earth and saw that men were very, very sinful.

God made us, and we ought to serve Him. But in those days men forgot all about God. They just did whatever they wanted to do. They did not love God. They did not even think about Him. They did not try to do what is right.

Then God said, "I will send a flood. I will send a great flood to wash all these sinful people off the earth."

So God spoke to Noah. He said to Noah, "Make a big boat, an ark, for you and your family. It must be a very big boat, three stories high. It must have a roof, and a window and a door. Make many little rooms inside the boat. And put tar on the inside and outside. Fill all the cracks with tar. For I am going to send a great flood. You and your family will be safe inside the ark when the flood comes."

Noah went to work. He cut wood. He sawed and he hammered. He worked day after day. Shem, Ham, and Japheth, his three sons, helped him. It took a long, long time to build the big ark.

Sometimes people came to watch Noah. Then he told them about the flood that was coming. But they laughed at him. They would not pray to God to save them from the flood.

At last the ark was finished. Then God told Noah to bring food into the ark — food for Noah and his family, and food for the animals. For God wanted to save animals alive, too.

Noah and his sons carried bushels and bushels of food into the ark.

Then the animals began to come. God sent them, two by two. A father and mother of each kind came to Noah. And of some kinds God sent seven.

At last God said, "Now take your wife and your sons, and your sons' wives. It is time to go into the ark."

Noah did just what God told him. He went into the ark, with his wife and his sons and their wives. Just eight people went in. And then God closed the door.

After a while, big black clouds began to cover the blue sky. The whole sky became dark. Then the rain began to fall. It fell faster and faster. Soon it came pouring down. And water began to come up from the ground, too.

It rained all day, and all night, and all the next day, and all the next day. It rained for forty days!

The city streets filled with water. The farms were covered with water. The water came higher and higher, up to the fence tops, up to the windows, up to the housetops, up to the treetops. It covered everything.

But the water lifted the ark. The ark floated on the flood.

All the animals and all the people left on earth were drowned. But Noah and his family were safe in the ark.

6

The Rainbow

(Genesis 8, 9)

The ark floated on the water for many, many days. When Noah and his sons looked out the window, they could see only water, water, everywhere. They could not see one house or one tree or one hilltop.

But God was watching the ark. He was taking care of Noah and his family. Soon He made the water go down, down, down.

And one morning, when Noah looked out, he saw the tops of the highest hills.

After a while the ark came to rest on one of the hills.

Then, one day, Noah opened the window and let a dove fly out. He thought maybe the dove would find a tree to rest in, and would not come back.

But the dove did come back. Noah opened the window and took it inside the ark again.

Noah waited a week. Then he let the dove out again. This time the dove stayed away all day. At night it came back. And it carried a leaf in its bill. Then Noah knew that the water was down to the treetops.

Noah waited another week. He sent the dove out once more, and it did not come back. So Noah knew that the water was gone. And God told Noah that he could leave the ark.

What a happy day that was! Noah and his wife and his sons and their wives — they were all glad to step out upon the clean earth. And the animals — the big ones and the little ones and all the creeping things — they ran out to play in the green grass. The birds spread their wings. They flew up into the blue sky. They sang their happy songs of praise to God.

Noah wanted to bring a gift to God. He wanted to thank God for saving them from the great flood. So he took big stones and made an altar. He took some of the animals that God sent into the ark by sevens. These he offered to God upon the altar.

Then God came to talk with Noah. God said, "I promise never to send such a flood again. Never again will I cover the whole earth with water. And I have put the sign of this promise in the sky."

Noah looked at the sky, and there he saw a rainbow. It was a beautiful rainbow, with brightest colors.

"That is the sign of my promise," said God.

And never again has there been a flood like that.

18

God told Noah he could leave the
ark. What a happy day that was!

7

A Friend of God

(*Genesis 12-17*)

The years went by. There were very many people upon the earth. They built houses and lived in big cities. Many had big farms. There were rich people and poor people.

But only a few people remembered God. Only a few people prayed to God.

There was a man named Abram. He lived in a country called Ur of the Chaldees. Abram prayed to God. Abram brought gifts to God upon his altar. And God called Abram His friend.

One day God said to Abram, "Abram, come out of the country where you live. Move to a country that I will show you. I will bless you. I will make a great nation of you. All the families of the earth shall be blessed in you."

What did God mean when He said, "All families of the earth shall be blessed in you"? He meant that He would give Abram a child and grandchildren and great-grandchildren, till at last one of them would be Mary. And Mary's son was Jesus, who came to save us from sin.

Abram did not understand all about this. But he did love God. He did want God to bless him.

So Abram told his servants to get ready to move. He told his wife, Sarai, to get ready. He took all the gold and silver that he had. He took all his sheep and cows and camels. Abram was a rich man.

Abram told Lot, his nephew, that he was going to move. Lot said he wanted to go along. Lot took all his sheep and cows and camels.

They had to go slowly. The sheep could not go fast. God led them to the land of Canaan.

In the land of Canaan Abram and Lot put up their tents. Abram made a new altar and brought his gifts to God on the altar. They lived in tents in the beautiful land of Canaan.

After a while Lot moved away from Abram. Lot went to live in the big city of Sodom.

One night Abram was sitting alone. He was thinking of God. He was thinking of God's promise. How could he ever have grandchildren? He did not have even one child.

Then God came to Abram. God said to Abram, "Come with me out under the sky."

Abram went with God into the dark night.

God said to him, "Now look up at the heavens. See if you can count the stars."

Abram looked up. The stars were shining bright. Some were very large and beautiful; some were smaller; some were so far away that Abram could hardly see them. There were very, very many.

"Can you count them?" God asked.

Abram shook his head. Count them? How could he count all those stars? There are so very, very many stars. Only God knows how many there are.

Then God said, "Your children's children shall be like that. There will be so many, that they cannot be counted."

Abram and Sarai had been married a long time. Yet they did not have even one child. But Abram believed God. He waited for God to keep His promise.

God talked to Abram again. He said, "After this your name shall be Abraham. That means 'Father of many.' And Sarai's name shall be Sarah. That means 'Princess.' And when your child comes, you must call him Isaac."

8

Abraham and Isaac

(*Genesis 22*)

Abraham and Sarah had a little baby at last — a little boy. They called him Isaac. That was the name God gave him.

Abraham and Sarah loved Isaac very much. He grew to be a very fine boy. He made them happy. They knew he was the beginning of the great nation that God had promised — a nation like the stars in number.

Many, many years later, Jesus, our Saviour, was born into this great nation which God had promised Abraham.

Then one day God called to Abraham.

Abraham answered, "Here I am, Lord."

God said to Abraham, "Take your son, your son Isaac, the son you love so much. Take him up to a mountain that I will show you. There you must make an altar. You must offer your son on the altar as a gift to me."

Abraham had made many altars. He had killed many sheep to burn as gifts to God. But now God asked for his son, his boy Isaac! And Abraham loved his boy so very, very much!

Next morning Abraham was up early. He cut some wood for a fire. He put some coals of fire in a jug. He took a big knife. All this he tied to a donkey. Then he called two of his servants, and Isaac. He told them to get ready to go along.

They traveled all day — Abraham and Isaac, the two servants, and the donkey. At night they slept under the stars. They traveled all the next day. And on the third day God showed them the mountain.

Then Abraham took the wood off the donkey. He gave it to Isaac, to carry on his back. Abraham took the coals of fire and the big knife himself.

Abraham said to the servants, "You stay here. The boy and I are going to worship God on the mountain. We will be back."

So Abraham and Isaac walked up the mountain together.

Isaac said to Abraham, "Father, we have wood and fire, but where is the lamb to burn?"

Abraham said, "God will take care of the lamb for us."

On the mountain Abraham built an altar of stones. He laid the wood on the altar. Then he tied Isaac with a rope, the way he always tied the sheep for sacrifice. He put Isaac on the altar and took the big knife in his hand. He lifted the knife high . . .

Then a voice called from heaven, "Abraham! Abraham!"

Abraham said, "Here I am!"

God's voice said, "Do not hurt the boy. Now I know that you love me. You were willing to give me your only son."

Then Abraham was very happy. He quickly took Isaac off the altar. They found a sheep in the bushes. So they gave the sheep to God instead of Isaac, on the altar.

Then Abraham and Isaac went down the mountain together. And Abraham loved God more than ever. For God had given Isaac to him twice.

9

God Answers Prayer

(*Genesis 24*)

Abraham was an old man. Isaac, his son, was grown up. But Isaac did not have a wife.

One day Abraham called his oldest servant. He said to the servant, "I do not want Isaac to marry one of the girls of this country. These girls do not serve God. I want you to go to my country, where I used to live. Go to my people, and find a good girl for Isaac."

The old servant said, "Your country is far away. Maybe the girl will not come with me, so far from home."

Abraham said, "If the girl will not come, then you must come back alone. But God will guide you to the right place."

So the old servant made ready. He took money, and he took beautiful gifts. He loaded ten camels, and rode away.

It was a long, long journey. When at last the old servant came to the country where Abraham used to live, he sat down by a well. He made his camels kneel there to rest.

Then the old servant bowed his head to pray. He said, "O God, by and by people will come to the well to let their sheep drink. Show me the girl who must be Isaac's wife. I will ask a girl for a drink. If she says, 'I will give your camels water, too,' let that be the right girl."

When the old man finished his prayer, he looked up and saw a girl come. She carried a pitcher on her shoulder. The old servant saw that she was a beautiful girl.

The old servant went to meet her. He said to her, "Will you please give me a drink?"

"Oh, yes," said the girl.

She went down to the well and filled her pitcher. She gave the old servant a drink. Then she said, "I will give your camels water, too." And she hurried to fill the pitcher again and again.

So the old man knew that this was the girl for Isaac. God had answered his prayer.

When all the camels had had enough water, the old man gave the girl a silver ring and two bracelets. Then he said, "Tell me who you are."

She said, "I am Rebekah. My grandfather is Nahor."

Nahor was Abraham's brother. This girl was truly one of Abraham's people.

The old servant went home with the girl. He told her family how Abraham had sent him. And he told how God answered his prayer. And the very next day Rebekah went with him. She became Isaac's wife.

10

Jacob and Esau
(*Genesis 25-27*)

Jacob and Esau were twin brothers.

But they were not one bit alike. Jacob had smooth skin. Esau had rough, hairy skin. Jacob loved to take care of sheep, and do little things around the house. Esau loved to go hunting with his bow and arrows.

In that long-ago time, a father always gave his oldest son a special blessing. When the father was old, he would call his oldest son and bless him. Jacob and Esau were twins, but Esau was just a little older than Jacob. So the blessing would be his. When their father Isaac was old, he would bless Esau.

But Jacob wanted the blessing.

One day Jacob was making soup. He stirred the soup over the fire, by his tent.

Esau came home from the hunt. He was tired and hungry. When he saw the soup, he wanted some.

"Let me have some of that soup," he said to Jacob.

Jacob said, "I will. But then you must give me the blessing."

Esau said, "What good is the blessing? I'm hungry now. You can have the blessing. I want the soup."

So Esau sold his blessing to Jacob, for some soup.

After a while, Isaac was old and blind. He knew he would soon die. So he called Esau.

Isaac said to Esau, "I am old, my son. I want to give you the blessing now. Go hunt a deer and bring me some meat. Then I will bless you."

Esau hurried away to get the deer. He wanted the blessing, after all.

But mother Rebekah heard all that Isaac said. She went to call Jacob. She told Jacob to hurry and get a little goat.

Rebekah quickly fixed the goat meat. She said to Jacob, "Bring this to your father. Tell him you are Esau. Then he will give you the blessing."

Jacob said, "But my father will feel my hands. My hands are smooth. Esau's hands are hairy."

Rebekah quickly took the skin of the goat. She put the hairy skin on Jacob's hands. She told Jacob to put on Esau's clothes. Then Jacob took the meat to Isaac's tent.

At the door of the tent Jacob called, "My father!"

Isaac answered, "Who are you, my son?"

Jacob said, "I am Esau. I brought the meat you asked for."

Isaac said, "You came back very soon."

Jacob said, "God helped me in the hunt."

But Isaac was not sure that it was Esau. He said, "Come near, so that I can feel you."

Jacob went near his father's bed. And Isaac felt of his hands. "The voice is Jacob's," he said. "But the skin is hairy like Esau's."

Then he took the meat and ate it.

When he had eaten the meat, he told Jacob to come near again. Then Isaac smelled the clothes. They smelled like the woods, where Esau loved to hunt.

And Isaac gave Jacob the blessing. He promised Jacob wonderful blessings from God.

As soon as he had the blessing, Jacob hurried away. Then Esau came.

Esau stood at the tent door. He called, "My father!"

Isaac said, "Who are you, my son?"

Esau said, "I am your son Esau. I have brought the meat you asked for."

Isaac said, "But who was here just now? I gave him the blessing!"

Then Esau knew that Jacob had cheated him. Esau was very angry. Esau was so angry that Jacob was afraid.

Rebekah said to Jacob, "You must go away. Go to my people, far away from here. Stay there until Esau is no longer angry."

So Jacob said goodbye to his father and mother. He went away from home, to a far country.

11

Jacob Finds a New Home

(*Genesis 28, 29*)

Jacob had a long, long way to go. He walked and walked through lonely country. And at night he lay down to sleep under the stars, with a stone for a pillow.

That night Jacob had a dream. In the dream, he saw a big ladder. The ladder stood on the earth. It reached

up to heaven. Bright angels were walking up and down the ladder. And at the top of the ladder stood someone brighter than the angels. It was the Lord God Himself.

God spoke to Jacob from the top of the ladder. He said, "I am the God of Abraham, your grandfather, and of Isaac, your father. I will be your God, too. I will give you this land where you are now. I will give it to you and to your children. And I will go with you, wherever you go."

Jacob awoke, and the ladder was gone. It had been only a dream ladder.

But Jacob knew that God really had talked to him in the dream. That made him afraid. But it made him happy, too.

Jacob said, "God is here. He sees me."

Then he took the stone he had used for a pillow. He set it up and poured oil on it. The oil was his thanksgiving to God.

Jacob said, "If God goes with me and takes care of me, I will serve Him. I will give Him a tenth part of all that He gives me."

Jacob went on then. God guided him along the way. By and by he came to a well. A big stone cover lay on the well.

There were shepherds sitting by the well. And flocks of sheep lay in the green grass around the well.

Jacob said to the shepherds, "Do you know Laban?"

The shepherds said, "Yes, we know him. He lives near here. And there comes his daughter, Rachel."

Jacob was glad to know Laban lived near. Laban was his uncle. So Jacob watched the girl come. She was bringing the sheep to the well for water.

When Rachel came near, Jacob took the big stone off the well. He helped Rachel give the sheep water. Then he told her that he was her cousin.

At the well, Jacob met Rachel
and helped water the sheep.

Rachel was glad to meet her cousin Jacob. She ran home to tell her father. Laban, Rachel's father, soon came running to see Jacob. He threw his arms around Jacob and kissed him.

"Come with me and live at my house," he said. "My house shall be your home."

So Jacob went with Laban. God had guided him to a new home.

Jacob worked for Laban many years. And at last he married the beautiful Rachel.

12

Joseph, the Dreamer
(Genesis 37)

Jacob put up his tents in the land of Canaan. He lived there with his big family. Jacob's twelve sons grew up. They helped to take care of the sheep.

Jacob loved Joseph best of all his sons. He loved Benjamin very much too. Benjamin was the youngest. But he loved Joseph best of all.

One day Jacob gave Joseph a beautiful coat. It was a coat of many bright colors. Joseph was happy with the coat. He liked to wear it.

But Joseph's brothers were angry. They said, "Our father does not give us such pretty things." And they began to hate Joseph.

Once Joseph dreamed a strange dream. In the dream he and his brothers were out in the field. They were cutting grain. Each one had a sheaf of ripe grain. And the sheaves of the brothers all bowed down before Joseph's sheaf.

Joseph told his brothers the dream. They said, "Do you think that we shall all bow down before you?" And they were more angry than ever.

Joseph's brothers were shepherds. Often they went far away from home to find grass for their sheep. One day Joseph's father sent Joseph to find them.

Joseph went a long way to find his brothers. And they saw him come. They said, "Here comes the dreamer. Look, he is wearing his beautiful coat of many colors."

Then they were angry again. One said, "Let's kill him."

When Joseph came near, the brothers took hold of him. They pulled off his coat. And they threw him down into a deep well.

There was no water in the well. But it was a deep, dark hole. Joseph begged his brothers to take him out.

One of the older brothers felt sorry for Joseph. That was Reuben. He thought, "When nobody is watching, I will take him out."

But after a while some men came along, riding on camels. Joseph's brothers saw them come. They said, "Let's not kill Joseph. Let's sell him to these men."

Reuben was gone just then. So the other brothers took Joseph out of the well. They sold him to be a slave. The men with camels gave them money and took Joseph away.

When Reuben came back, he looked into the well. Joseph was not there! His brothers told Reuben what they had done.

Reuben said, "What will we tell our father?"

The brothers said, "We will kill a goat and put blood on Joseph's coat. We will send the coat to our father. Then he will think that a wild animal killed Joseph."

They did kill a goat. They spattered blood on Joseph's coat. When father Jacob saw Joseph's coat, all spattered with blood, he said, "Joseph is dead! A wild animal surely killed him!" And he was very sad.

But the men with the camels took Joseph far away, to Egypt. There they sold Joseph to be the slave of a rich man.

13

Joseph in Prison

(*Genesis 39, 40*)

Joseph worked hard in Egypt. He did his best to serve his master. And God blessed Joseph.

Then, one day, Joseph's master believed a lie about Joseph. He put Joseph in prison. But God was with Joseph in prison, too.

After a while, the great Pharaoh, king of Egypt, sent two men to prison. They were the king's butler and his baker.

Every day Joseph talked with the butler and the baker. One morning he found them looking very sad.

Joseph said, "What makes you look so sad this morning?"

They said, "We had such strange dreams last night! We are sure the dreams mean something."

Joseph said, "Tell me the dreams."

The butler told his dream. He said, "I saw a grape vine with three branches. Leaves and flowers began to grow on the branches, and then grapes grew. When the grapes were ripe, I picked them. I squeezed the juice into Pharaoh's cup. And I brought the cup to Pharaoh."

Then God told Joseph the meaning of the dream. Joseph said to the butler, "The three branches are three days. After three days Pharaoh will take you out of prison. You will be his butler again."

That made the butler very happy.

Joseph said, "When you see Pharaoh again, tell him about me. Maybe he will take me out of prison, too."

Then the baker told his dream. He said, "I had three baskets on my head, one on top of the other. In the baskets there was bread and cake for Pharaoh. But the birds came and ate it."

Joseph said, "The three baskets mean three days. After three days Pharaoh will take you out of prison. But he will not make you his baker again. He will hang you. And the birds will come to peck at you."

That made the baker very sad.

And the dreams came true. After three days, Pharaoh took the butler and the baker out of prison. He hanged the baker. He took the butler back to the palace, to pour his wine again.

But the butler forgot all about Joseph.

14

Joseph in the Palace

(Genesis 41)

The great Pharaoh, king of Egypt, lived in a beautiful palace. He had many servants and many wise men.

One night, as Pharaoh lay asleep in his beautiful bed, he had a strange dream. He stood by the river and saw seven fat cows come out of the water. Then seven thin cows came out. The thin cows ate up the fat cows. And still they were thin.

He had another dream. He saw a tall corn plant with seven big ears of corn. There was another corn plant with seven thin ears of corn. The seven thin ears swallowed up the seven big ears. And still they were thin.

Pharaoh awoke and said, "What a strange dream! It must surely have a special meaning!"

So he called his wise men. He told them the dream. But they could not tell the meaning.

Just then the butler came with Pharaoh's wine. He heard about the dream. And he said, "O king, I know a man who can tell the meaning of dreams. His name is Joseph. He is in prison. When Pharaoh put me in prison, I had a dream. This Joseph told me the meaning. And it came true, just as he said."

Then Pharaoh quickly sent for Joseph.

Joseph washed himself, and put on clean clothes, and hurried to the palace. There he bowed low before Pharaoh.

Pharaoh said to Joseph, "I have heard that you can tell the meaning of dreams."

But Joseph said, "Only God knows the meaning of dreams."

Then Pharaoh told the dream — about the thin cows and the fat cows, and about the thin ears of corn and the fat ones.

Joseph said, "God sent that dream to Pharaoh to tell what is going to happen. Then seven thin cows ate up the seven fat cows; the seven thin ears swallowed up the seven fat ears. That means there will be seven years of plenty. Corn and wheat and barley will grow better than ever before. But then seven years of famine will come. The seven years of famine will eat up all you save in the seven years of plenty."

Pharaoh listened carefully. Then he said, "Who is wiser than Joseph? Let Joseph take care of the food, to save it for the seven years of famine."

So Pharaoh made Joseph governor of Egypt. He gave him a beautiful ring, and a chain of gold, and the very best clothes. He told all the people to obey Joseph. And Joseph lived like a king in the land of Egypt.

15

Joseph's Brothers

(Genesis 42)

There was famine in all the lands around Egypt. But in Egypt there was plenty of food. Joseph, the great governor of Egypt, had filled the barns with wheat and corn and barley. So from all the lands around, people came to Joseph to buy food.

One day ten men came from a far country. They wanted to buy food. They bowed low before Joseph.

Joseph looked at them, and he saw that they were his own brothers! Long ago these brothers had sold Joseph to be a slave in Egypt. Now he was governor. And they did not know him.

Joseph made believe he did not know them. He looked angry and said, "Who are you?"

They said, "We are sons of a man who lives in Canaan. We came to buy food. We have one more brother at home."

Joseph said to them, "You are bad men. You are spies. I shall put you all in prison."

And that is what he did.

The ten brothers were sad in prison. They thought of their poor father. And they thought of Joseph. They remembered how he had cried when they sold him to strange men.

After three days, Joseph let them out of prison. He said to them, "Nine of you may go home. One must go back to prison. And when you come again, you must bring your youngest brother. Don't you dare come without him."

So nine of the brothers went home. They were sad. They said to each other, "This has happened to us because we sold our brother Joseph."

They had to tell father Jacob all that happened. They told him about the hard governor, and how Simeon was in prison, and that they had to take Benjamin along next time.

Then Jacob shook his head. He said, "Joseph is gone, and Simeon is gone, and must you take Benjamin away too? If anything happens to Benjamin, I shall die of sorrow."

16

Joseph and Jacob Meet Again

(*Genesis 43-46*)

Once again Joseph's brothers went to Egypt for food. They took Benjamin, the youngest, along. The governor of Egypt had said, "Don't you dare come again without Benjamin."

They came to the great governor. They bowed low before him. They did not know he was their own brother.

Joseph, the governor, said to his servant, "Take these men to my house. Make a dinner for them."

The servant made dinner. Then he told each man where to sit. He made them sit in a row, the oldest first and the youngest last. Simeon came out of prison to have dinner, too.

Joseph's brothers thought, "How does this man know who is oldest, and who is next oldest, and next oldest?" But they did not dare ask.

The next day, Joseph told them they could all go

How glad Jacob was to see his son Joseph again!

home. How glad they were to get away! Their sacks of grain were all ready. They loaded their donkeys and rode away.

But Joseph had told his servant to put Joseph's silver cup in Benjamin's sack.

When the brothers were riding along, they heard somebody on a horse galloping behind them. They looked, and they saw the governor's servant.

He looked very angry. He caught up with them and said, "How did you dare to steal my master's cup?"

Joseph's brothers said, "Oh no, we would not do such a thing! You may look in all our sacks. If you find the cup, we will all go back. We will be slaves of your master."

The servant of the governor said, "If I find the cup, the man who has it will be my master's slave."

Then he began to hunt. He opened Reuben's sack first. Reuben was the oldest. Then he opened the next sack, and the next. The silver cup was not in them. At last he opened Benjamin's sack. And there it was! Benjamin would have to be a slave!

The brothers said, "We will all go back with Benjamin."

Very sadly they went back to Egypt, to the hard governor.

Joseph, the governor, said, "No, I do not want you all to be slaves. I want only Benjamin. The rest of you may go home."

Then Judah, one of the brothers, said, "Please take me instead of Benjamin. Our father loves Benjamin very, very much. He will die if Benjamin does not come back. Take me, and let Benjamin go home."

Judah told about Joseph. He said, "Once we had another brother. My father loved him very much. But Joseph is gone. My father cannot bear to lose Benjamin, too."

Then Joseph could not keep his secret any longer. He cried out, "I am your brother! I am Joseph!"

How surprised the brothers were! They could hardly believe it! But Joseph told them how God had blessed him, and how God had made him governor of Egypt.

They talked a long time. Then Joseph said, "Go get our father. Tell him Joseph is alive. Tell him to come to me."

The brothers hurried home. And Joseph sent a chariot for his old father to ride in.

So Jacob came to Egypt. Joseph rode to meet him. When they met, they threw their arms around each other and wept for joy.

Jacob lived to be an old man. When he died, he thanked God for leading him all through his life so wonderfully.

17

A Baby in a Basket

(Genesis 49; Exodus 1, 2)

Jacob and his sons, and all their children, lived in Egypt for many years. Jacob became very old. Then he called all his sons to his bedside. He told them that God would some day bring them back to Canaan. And he told them that some day God would send a Saviour.

Then Jacob blessed his sons. And he died.

After a while Joseph and his brothers died, too. God took them away, one by one.

The children of Joseph and of his brothers lived in Egypt. There were very many children. God blessed them. They became a great nation. They were called the children of Israel.

Then there was another Pharaoh. The new Pharaoh did not like the children of Israel. He said, "There are too many of them."

This Pharaoh made the children of Israel his slaves. He made them work very hard. They had to make bricks. They had to build cities with the bricks. They worked very, very hard.

Pharaoh also made a cruel law. The law said that every baby boy must be thrown into the river to drown.

One day a very dear baby boy was born. His mother and father loved the baby. They would not throw him into the river.

The mother hid the baby. She kept him a long time.

But after a while the mother did not dare keep the baby any longer. He was three months old. Sometimes he cried very loud. Pharaoh's soldiers would surely hear him.

The mother thought and thought about it. One morning she went to the river and picked some reeds. She took the reeds home. She wove the reeds into a basket.

She made the basket very strong. When it was finished, she filled all the cracks with pitch. Then it was like a little boat.

The mother made a bed in the little basket. She put the baby in it, and covered him carefully. Then she took the basket to the river.

The baby's sister, Miriam, went along.

At the edge of the river they put the basket down. It rocked on the little waves among the reeds. The mother did not want it to float away. So Miriam stayed to watch. And the mother went home.

Miriam hid in the bushes. After a while she heard voices. She saw ladies come to the river. It was the princess, Pharaoh's daughter. She and her maids were coming to bathe in the river.

Would they see the basket? Miriam watched. One of the maids walked near the basket. Then she ran back to the princess to tell her something. And Miriam heard the princess say, "Go and get it."

The maid got the basket, and Miriam watched her bring it to the princess. She saw the princess lift the cover. And she heard the baby cry.

Then the princess said, "It is one of the babies of the children of Israel." And Miriam knew that she felt sorry for the baby.

So Miriam came out of her hiding place and went to the princess. She said, "Shall I find a nurse to take care of the baby?"

The princess said, "Yes, go. Find a nurse."

Miriam ran home. "Oh, Mother!" she said, "the princess found the basket! And she wants a nurse!"

Miriam's mother hurried back with Miriam.

The princess said, "Take this baby home with you. Take care of him for me. I will pay you. When he is old enough, bring him to me."

How happy the mother was! She bowed to the princess, and hurried home with her baby.

She loved her baby. She took good care of him. She taught him about God.

But when he was old enough, she had to give him to the princess. She brought him to the palace. The princess called him Moses, and said that he was her boy.

18

The Burning Bush

(*Exodus 2, 3, 4*)

Moses lived with the princess until he was a man. He went to school in the palace. He learned all the wisdom of Egypt. But he did not forget God.

All this time Pharaoh was cruel. He made the children of Israel work very hard. They were his slaves.

44

Moses wanted to help the children of Israel. He did not want to live in the palace while they worked so hard. But he did not know how to help them. So he ran away to the country. He became a shepherd.

One day, when Moses was with the sheep, he saw a burning bush. The bush burned and burned, but it did not burn up. That seemed very strange. Moses went near the bush to see it better.

Then suddenly Moses heard a voice call, "Moses! Moses!"

Moses looked around. He did not see anyone. But he said, "Here I am!"

Then the voice said, "Do not come near to the bush. Take your shoes off your feet, for you are standing on holy ground."

Moses took off his shoes. He knew it must be God who spoke to him. He knew it must be God who made the bush burn so strangely. He put his hands over his face.

God said to him, "I am the God of Abraham, Isaac and Jacob. The children of Israel are my people. They cry to me because Pharaoh makes them work very hard. Now I have come to help them."

Moses listened. He was glad that God had come to help His people.

God said, "I shall bring them to the land of Canaan. And I have chosen you, Moses, to take them out of Egypt."

Then Moses said, "Oh, no! Do not ask me to do that! How can I do that? They will not follow me. And Pharaoh will not listen to me."

God said to him, "I will go with you. I will bring them to a beautiful land."

But Moses was afraid. He said, "The people will not believe me. They will not believe that God talked to me."

Then God gave Moses two wonderful signs to show the people and said, "When you talk to the children of Israel, you can do those two signs. Then they will believe that I sent you."

And God promised to send Moses' brother, Aaron, to help him.

So Moses brought his sheep home, and he went to Egypt.

19

Pharaoh Says "No" to God

(*Exodus 5, 6*)

Moses went to Egypt. On the way he met Aaron. God had sent Aaron to meet Moses. Then Moses and Aaron went on to Egypt together.

Moses and Aaron went to the children of Israel first.

The children of Israel had not heard about God for a long, long time. They did not have a Bible. They thought God had forgotten them.

Moses told them that God was going to help them, that God was going to take them out of Egypt, that God would give them a beautiful land to live in.

Then Moses showed them the two signs.

He threw his rod on the ground. It became a snake. He picked it up, and it became a rod again.

After that, he put his hand inside his coat. When he took it out, all the children of Israel saw that it was white like snow. Then he put his hand inside his coat again, and it became well.

So the children of Israel knew that God had sent Moses. And they were very happy. They wanted to get away from cruel Pharaoh.

Then Moses and Aaron went to Pharaoh. They told Pharaoh what God had said.

Pharaoh said, "Who is God? I do not know Him. I will not let the children of Israel go!"

Pharaoh sent Moses and Aaron away. He was angry. He made the children of Israel work harder.

Moses felt sorry for the people. They worked so very, very hard. Moses prayed to God. He said, "O God, Pharaoh will not let the people go. He makes them work harder than before I spoke to him."

But God said, "I am God Almighty. I will bring my people to Canaan. But first I will show Pharaoh great wonders."

20

God Sets His People Free

(Exodus 6-12)

The great Pharaoh sat upon his throne. Before him stood a shepherd, with a staff in his hand. The shepherd was Moses. And his brother Aaron was with him.

Moses said to Pharaoh, "The Lord God has sent me. He sent me to lead His people out of Egypt."

But Pharaoh was angry. He said to Moses, "I do not know the Lord God. I will not let the people go."

Aaron threw down the staff before Pharaoh, and it turned into a snake. But still Pharaoh would not listen. He would not let God's people go.

God said to Moses, "I will send great plagues upon Pharaoh. Then at last he will let my people go."

God sent terrible plagues. He turned the water of the river into blood, so that the people of Egypt did not have water to drink. He sent frogs; the frogs came into the houses of the Egyptians, and into their beds, and into their ovens. He sent lice to crawl on men and animals. He sent swarms of flies that buzzed everywhere. He sent sickness upon the cattle.

But Pharaoh would not let God's people go.

Then God sent more plagues. He sent boils on the people of Egypt. He sent a storm, with hailstones and thunder and lightning. He sent grasshoppers to eat up all the green things. He sent three days of darkness, so that the people could not see at all.

But still Pharaoh would not let God's people go.

At last God sent an angel — an Angel of Death. The Angel of Death killed Pharaoh's oldest son. And he killed the oldest son of every house in Egypt. But the Angel of Death passed over the houses of God's people.

Then Pharaoh called Moses. He told Moses to go away, to hurry away, with all God's people.

It was night. But the people were ready. God had told them to be ready. Moses and Aaron led them out.

The people carried tents to live in. They carried their beds, and their clothes, and all that they had. And the people of Egypt gave them gold and silver to take along.

So they marched out of Egypt — mothers and fathers, boys and girls, little babies that had to be carried, and a long line of sheep and cattle. The people were all happy. They had been Pharaoh's slaves for a long, long time. Now they were free. So they praised God as they marched out of Egypt.

48

21

A Path Through the Sea

(*Exodus 14*)

God's people of long ago were called Israelites. God did many wonderful things for the Israelites. He took them out of Egypt. And He brought them to a beautiful new home called Canaan.

It was a long journey to Canaan. God led them with a great Cloud. The Cloud was like a pillar. It moved ahead of the Israelites. When the Cloud stopped, they stopped.

One day the Cloud stopped by a lake called the Red Sea. The Israelites put up their tents. They made their dinner. After dinner they put the children to bed.

But then they heard a noise. It was a noise like thunder. Pharaoh was coming! He was coming, with all his soldiers, to take the Israelites back to Egypt! Then the people were afraid.

But Moses, their leader, said, "Do not be afraid. Just be still and see what God will do for you."

Pharaoh and the soldiers came nearer and nearer. And then the Cloud began to move. The Cloud moved around the camp, until it was behind the tents. It was between the Israelites and the Egyptians. The Egyptians could not come near the Israelites.

When night came, the Cloud was like a pillar of fire. It gave light to the Israelites.

Then God spoke to Moses. He told Moses to hold his staff out over the water of the Red Sea.

Moses did just what God told him to do. And when he held his staff over the sea, an east wind began to blow. The east wind blew all night long. It piled the

By night God led them
with the Pillar of Fire.

51

water into two high walls. God used the wind to blow a path right through the Red Sea.

The Israelites took their tents down. They walked into the Red Sea, on a dry path, between the two walls of water. They walked all the way across. So God brought them safely to the other side of the Red Sea.

The Egyptians tried to follow the Israelites. But God made the path muddy for them. They could not get through the mud. And when all the people of God were safe on the other side, God let the two walls of water tumble down. The water splashed right down upon the Egyptians, and drowned them.

Then Miriam, Moses' sister, played her timbrel. And all the people of God sang praises to Him. For He saved them from the Egyptians.

And He led them on to their new home. By day He led them with the Cloud. By night He led them with the Pillar of Fire.

22

The Shining Serpent
(*Numbers 21*)

It was a long, long journey to Canaan. The Israelites had to go through dry deserts and over high hills. But God took care of them. He gave them water out of a rock. He gave them bread from heaven. Each morning, except on the Sabbath day, the bread lay upon the ground. They called it manna.

But the Israelites were tired of traveling. They were tired of the manna. They began to grumble and complain.

God heard them grumble and complain. He saw that they were cross and angry. And one day God sent serpents into the camp, to punish the Israelites who grumbled.

The serpents crawled all around the camp, between the tents. They bit many people. Many people died of the poison bites.

Then the Israelites called to Moses, their leader. They said, "We have sinned. It was sinful to grumble and complain. Pray to God, so that He will take the serpents away."

Moses did pray. And God said to Moses, "Make a serpent of shining brass. Put it on a high pole. And tell the people to look at the shining serpent. When they look at the shining serpent, they will be well."

Moses quickly made the serpent of shining brass. He put it on a pole, so high that people could see it from afar.

Many people were very sick from the serpent bites — mothers, and fathers, and little children, too. They all heard about the shining serpent. And when they looked at it, they were well. They did not die.

Then the people thanked God for the shining serpent.

Many, many years later Jesus was lifted high upon the cross. And whosoever believes on Him is made well from all sins.

23

The Walls of Jericho

(Joshua 6)

There once was a big city called Jericho. The people who lived in Jericho were wicked people. They did not serve the Lord. They did not try to do His will.

So God said that He would punish them. He would give their city to His own people.

But all around the city of Jericho there was a big high wall — a very strong wall. And the people of Jericho shut the gates of the city tight. They would not let anyone come in or go out. They saw the people of God outside the city, and they were afraid.

Joshua was then the leader of God's people. And God told Joshua what to do.

Joshua called the priests and all the soldiers. He told them to get in line. He said they were going to march all around the city.

First in line were soldiers, hundreds of them. Then came seven priests. Each priest had a horn to blow. Then came four priests, carrying God's ark. And at the end of the line the rest of the soldiers marched.

When they were all ready, the seven priests blew their horns. Everybody began to march. Nobody talked. They only marched — tramp, tramp, tramp.

They marched all the way around Jericho. Then they went back to their tents.

The next day they did the same — tramp, tramp, tramp around the city. And the next day they did the same, for six days.

On the seventh day they were up early. Joshua said they must march around the city seven times that day. He said that then God would give them the city.

Early in the morning they started — tramp, tramp, tramp. The priests blew their horns. But nobody talked. They marched around and around and around, seven times.

Then Joshua gave the signal, and all the soldiers shouted. They shouted as loud as they could.

And when they shouted, the walls of Jericho fell. The walls came crashing down. The soldiers could run right in and take the city.

So God gave the city of Jericho to His people.

24

Brave Gideon

(Judges 6, 7)

When God's people served Him, He blessed them. But there came a time when God's people forgot Him. They served other gods. Then God sent wicked men to punish them. These men stole the wheat and barley out of the fields.

Then the Israelites called to God. They asked God to forgive them and help them.

God heard their prayer. He forgave them. And He called Gideon to fight against the thieves.

Gideon was not a brave man. He was afraid to fight. He gathered a big army, and still he was afraid.

Then God said to Gideon, "Your army is too big." He let Gideon have just a little army.

But the enemies had a much bigger army. The valley was full of soldiers. No wonder Gideon was afraid!

But God told Gideon just what to do. In the night He said to Gideon, "Take one of your soldiers. Go down into the valley. Listen to what the men in the valley say."

Gideon and his soldier crept down the hill in the dark. They could see the great big army asleep in the valley. When they came near, they heard two soldiers talking. One said, "I had a strange dream. A loaf of bread came rolling down the hill. It knocked a tent down."

The other said, "That loaf of bread must be Gideon's army. God is going to give our whole army to Gideon."

When Gideon heard that, he knew God would help him. Then he was no longer afraid. With God helping him, he was brave.

Gideon hurried back up the hill. He woke his soldiers. He gave each one a trumpet, a water jar, and a
torch. They put their torches inside the water jars,
to hide the lights. Then they crept quietly around.
They made a circle all around the valley where the
big army of enemies was asleep.

They were all very quiet. And it was very dark.
Then Gideon gave the signal. The men took out their
torches and held them high. They threw down their
jars, crashing them against the rocks. They blew their
trumpets as loud as they could. And they shouted,
"The sword of the Lord and of Gideon!"

Such a bright light! And so much noise! The big
army in the valley scared awake. They did not know
what was happening. They jumped up and ran. And
Gideon's little army chased them.

So the Lord saved His people when they prayed to
Him.

25

Ruth Chooses for God

(*Ruth*)

Once upon a time there was a famine in the land of
Israel. The rain did not fall. The grain did not grow.
After a while there was not food enough.

Then a certain man, named Elimelech, moved away
to another country. He took Naomi, his wife, with him,
and their two boys.

The two boys grew up in the strange country. They
married two good girls — Ruth and Orpah.

But after a while Elimelech died. And the two boys
died. Naomi was alone with Ruth and Orpah.

Naomi was sad and lonely. She wanted to go back to her own country.

Ruth and Orpah walked along with Naomi. But after a while Naomi said, "You must go back to your own country. You must not come with me all the way."

So Orpah kissed Naomi. She said goodbye, and went back to her country. But Ruth did not want to go back.

Ruth said to Naomi, "I will go where you go. I will live where you live. Your people shall be my people. Your God shall be my God."

So Ruth chose for God. And she went with Naomi, to live with God's people.

When harvest time came, Ruth went out to pick up barley in the field. The reapers cut the barley, and tied it into bundles. But they dropped some of it. And the poor people could pick up all that the reapers dropped. Ruth followed the reapers all day. She took the barley home to Naomi.

The barley field belonged to a rich man, named Boaz. Boaz saw Ruth picking up barley. He talked with her. He said to her, "I have heard that you are good to Naomi. The Lord will bless you because you are good to her."

He told her to come every day. And he told the reapers to drop more barley for her.

So Ruth went to the fields of Boaz every day, till the harvest was past. And after that, the rich Boaz married Ruth. And God sent them a baby boy. This baby grew up and became the grandfather of great king David.

So God did bless Ruth, because she chose to serve Him, and because she was good to Naomi, her mother-in-law.

26

Samson, the Strong Man

(*Judges 13-16*)

Once again the Israelites forgot God. Then God sent the Philistines to bother them. And the people prayed to God for help.

God heard their prayers.

One day God sent an angel to a woman of Israel. The angel said, "You shall have a baby. And this baby will grow up to fight against the Philistines. But he must not drink wine. And he must never have his hair cut."

After a time, the baby came. He grew up to be a big strong man — bigger and stronger than other men. He did not drink wine. And he never had his hair cut. His name was Samson.

Samson was very strong. One day he met a lion on the path. He caught the lion by its mouth and killed it.

When the Philistines came, he chased them away. They were afraid of him.

One day the Philistines did catch Samson. They tied him with strong ropes. But Samson laughed. He just broke the ropes, and he walked away!

Samson had a friend whose name was Delilah. Delilah was not a good woman. But Samson often went to visit her.

One day the Philistines came to see Delilah. They said to her, "You must find out what makes Samson so strong. If you help us catch him, we will give you money."

So Delilah asked Samson what it was that made him strong.

Samson grew up to be very strong;
one day he killed a lion.

Samson did not want to tell. But Delilah begged and begged.

At last Samson told her how the angel had come to his mother. He told her that he had always obeyed God. He never drank wine. His hair had never been cut.

Then Delilah put Samson to sleep. And while he was asleep she cut off his long hair.

The Philistines were hiding near by.

Delilah woke Samson and said, "Samson, the Philistines are coming!"

Samson jumped up. He thought he was as strong as before. He thought he would chase the Philistines away.

But he was weak. He could not chase the Philistines. The Spirit of God had made him strong. But the Spirit of God left him, because he let Delilah cut his hair.

The Philistines took Samson to prison. They put his eyes out. And they made him work hard.

After a while Samson's hair grew long again. And one day the Philistines had a great feast. They were all in one big temple. And they brought Samson, so that they could make fun of him.

Then Samson prayed to God. He asked God to make him strong just once more.

God heard Samson's prayer. Samson put his arms around the pillars of the temple. On the roof above his head the Philistines were laughing and talking. Samson pulled hard. He pulled with all his might. The pillars cracked. They broke. The temple came tumbling down. It fell on many Philistines, and killed them.

Samson, too, was killed. But he freed the Israelites from the Philistines.

27

Samuel, the Temple Boy

(I Samuel 1)

Elkanah was a man who served God. Each year he went to bring a gift to God in His Tabernacle. The Tabernacle was like a church. The people worshipped God there.

Elkanah's wife, Hannah, went along to the Tabernacle. Hannah did not have children, and she wished she had a baby. So when she came to the Tabernacle with Elkanah, she asked God for a baby.

Hannah prayed for a long time. She prayed softly, just moving her lips. She said, "O Lord, if you will give me a son, I will give him back to Thee."

Near by, old priest Eli sat watching her. He did not know what she was doing. After a while he said to her, "Did you drink too much wine?"

Hannah said, "Oh no. I did not drink any wine. I was praying."

Then the old priest said, "And may God give you what you ask of Him."

Hannah went home with a happy heart. And before another year was gone, she had a baby boy.

Hannah named the baby Samuel.

When Samuel was still a very little boy, Elkanah and Hannah took him along to the Tabernacle. They brought him to the old priest, Eli.

Hannah said to Eli, "Do you remember me? Do you remember how I stood in the Tabernacle, praying? I asked God for a baby. And He gave me this little boy. Now I want to give my little boy to God."

When they went home, they left Samuel with Eli. He became a little temple boy, serving God every day in the Tabernacle.

When Samuel grew up, he became a great prophet. He led God's people in the ways of the Lord.

28

David, the Shepherd Boy

(*I Samuel 16*)

In the town of Bethlehem, long, long ago, there lived a boy named David. David was a shepherd boy. He loved to watch over the sheep. He led them in green pastures and he found cool water for them to drink. Many times David took his harp out to the hills. Then he played beautiful songs of praise to God, and he sang about the wonderful works of God.

One day a white-haired man came to Bethlehem. It was Samuel, the prophet.

The people were happy to see Samuel. They made a feast for him. Jesse, David's father, went to the feast. David's brothers went to the feast, too. But David was out in the hills, watching the sheep.

Samuel said to the people, "God sent me to anoint a king. It will be one of the sons of Jesse. I will pour oil on the head of the one God chooses. And some day he will be king of Israel."

Then the sons of Jesse came to Samuel. They walked by him, one by one. But Samuel shook his head. God did not choose one of them.

Samuel said to Jesse, "Is this all of your sons?"

Jesse said, "I have one more son. He is just a boy. He is out on the hills, watching the sheep."

Samuel said, "Call him to come."

Someone ran to find David. David hurried home. He washed and dressed. Then he went to the feast.

Samuel saw David coming. And the Lord said to Samuel, "This is the one. Anoint him. He will be king of Israel."

When David came near, Samuel poured the oil on his head. And the Spirit of God lived in David's heart ever after that.

But when the feast was over, David went back home. He took care of his father's sheep again.

29

David and the Giant

(*I Samuel 17*)

David's brothers were soldiers in the army. They went to fight against the Philistines. David was not old enough to be a soldier.

But one day David's father sent him to the army to see how his brothers were.

While David talked with his brothers, he heard a big voice cry out, "Send somebody to fight me! You say you have a great God. But you are afraid of me. Who dares to come and fight me?"

David looked around. And there, up on a hill, stood a big giant. He had a great big sword and a great big spear.

All the soldiers were afraid of the giant. They said, "Listen. That is Goliath, the giant. Nobody dares fight him."

David said, "Why does nobody dare fight him? We are God's people. We cannot let him make fun of our God."

Then the soldiers brought David to king Saul.

King Saul said, "Do you dare go fight the giant? You are not big enough!"

David said, "Once a bear caught a little lamb, and God helped me kill the bear. Once a lion came for a sheep, and God helped me kill the lion. He will help me kill this giant."

Then Saul let him go, to fight the giant.

David did not have a sword. He had his slingshot. He went to the creek and found five smooth stones. Then he went to meet the giant.

Goliath laughed when he saw David come. David was just a boy!

But David said, "I come in the name of the Lord!"

Then David put a stone in his slingshot. He ran, and he threw the stone. The stone hit Goliath in the forehead. And the big giant fell dead.

When the Philistines saw the giant fall, they ran. The men of Israel ran after them. They chased the Philistines out of the country.

Then all the people of Israel sang songs about David and the giant.

King Saul took David home, to live in the king's palace.

30

David Runs Away

(I Samuel 18-20)

Saul had a son named Jonathan. When David lived in the house of King Saul, David and Jonathan became friends.

But after a while Saul began to hate David. He hated David because he knew that some day David would be king.

Then it happened that Saul became very sick. An evil spirit came to bother him.

Saul's servants said, "Music will chase the evil spirit away. We must find someone who can play sweet music."

They knew David could play. So they called David to play his harp for Saul.

When David played his harp, the evil spirit went away.

After a while the evil spirit came to bother Saul again. The servants called David again, to play his beautiful music for Saul.

But this time the evil spirit did not go away. Saul looked at David and hated him more than ever. Suddenly Saul took his spear and threw it at David.

David saw the spear come. He stepped aside. And the spear went into the wall. But after that David could not play for Saul again. He was afraid Saul would kill him.

Jonathan said to David, "I do not think that my father really wants to harm you. I will ask him. If he does, I will help you run away."

So they made a plan. Jonathan said he would talk to King Saul.

Jonathan said, "When I come back, I will bring my bow and arrows, and I will bring my little boy. I will shoot an arrow, and tell my little boy to get it. If I shoot it just a little way, that means you can stay here. If I shoot it far, that means you must go away."

Jonathan went to talk to Saul. David hid in the bushes and waited.

Soon Jonathan came back. He had his bow and arrows. And the little boy was with him.

David watched Jonathan. He saw Jonathan take an arrow and shoot it. The arrow flew far away, out into the field.

Jonathan called to the little boy, "The arrow is far away! Run and get it!"

The little boy ran to get the arrow. Then Jonathan gave him the bow and arrows and sent him home.

When the little boy was gone, David came out of his hiding place. He knew he would have to go away. The arrow told him that.

Jonathan came to meet David. They kissed each other and said goodbye. They were sad. Then David went away into the wild country. He found a cave in the hills, and he lived in the cave. After a while other men came to live with David. They made David their leader.

31

David Becomes King

(*II Samuel 1, 5, 9*)

After a while, the Philistines made war again. Saul and his soldiers had to fight against the Philistines. Jonathan was a captain in the army. They all went out to fight a big battle.

The Philistines were strong. They won the battle. Saul and Jonathan were killed.

The news went through the land, the awful news — King Saul is killed, and Jonathan, his son, is killed. People were afraid. They did not know what would happen next. They did not have a king to lead them.

In Jonathan's house, a nurse was taking care of Jonathan's little boy. The boy's name was Mephibosheth.

The nurse did not know what to do. She picked up little Mephibosheth and started to run away. But she dropped him, and the fall hurt both his feet. After that, Mephibosheth could not walk well. But somebody took him and cared for him.

David heard about the battle, too. A messenger came and told him that Saul and Jonathan were dead.

Then David was very sad. He had loved Jonathan very much.

After a while David asked God, "Shall I go back to my own country now?"

God told him to go.

David went back to his own country. And the people made him king in Saul's place. At last the little shepherd boy became a king.

The people loved David. He was a good king. He did what was right.

One day David said, "Is there anybody left of Saul's family? If there is anybody, I want to be kind to him."

They told David about Mephibosheth.

David told his men to find Mephibosheth. They brought him to David. Mephibosheth was a cripple. He came to David and fell on his face before David.

David said to him, "Do not be afraid. Jonathan, your father, was my friend. I will be kind to you."

David gave Mephibosheth some servants and some land. And Mephibosheth ate at the king's table every day.

David lived in Jerusalem. He built a beautiful house there. And God blessed David.

32

Fire From Heaven

(*I Kings 18*)

Once upon a time there was a great famine in the land of Israel. For three long years there was no rain. The sun shone bright. The earth dried up. There were no gardens. Even the grass would not grow.

The famine was a punishment. Ahab, king of Israel, had made an idol, a god of stone. The idol's name was Baal. Ahab had priests to worship Baal. And he told all the people to pray to the idol.

The people did what Ahab told them to do. They worshipped the idol. They forgot God. And that is why God sent the famine.

But there was one good man — the prophet Elijah.

Elijah went to king Ahab. He said to king Ahab, "You are to blame for this awful famine. You led the people to serve Baal. Now call all the people together. We shall see if Baal is really a god."

So Ahab called all the people together. They came to a hill. Elijah waited there for them, early in the morning. A great crowd came, with four hundred and fifty prophets of Baal.

Elijah stood on the hillside. He said to all the people, "There are four hundred and fifty prophets of Baal. And I am the only prophet of the Lord. Today we shall see who is truly God. You pray to Baal. I will pray to the Lord. The one who sends fire from heaven, he is truly God."

The people said, "That is good. If Baal sends fire, we will know that he is a true god. If the Lord sends fire, we will know that He is God."

Elijah said, "The God who sends fire,
he will be the true God."

The prophets of Baal made their altar first. They put wood on it, and an ox to burn. Then they began to pray. They asked Baal to send fire.

But the fire did not come.

They prayed and prayed, louder and louder. Still fire did not come.

All morning long they prayed. Still fire did not come.

Elijah laughed at them. He said, "Maybe Baal is sleeping!"

The priests of Baal began jumping up and down. They prayed louder. They cut themselves with knives. Still Baal did not send fire.

Then Elijah said, "It is my turn now. Come near and watch."

The people watched. Elijah made an altar of stones. He dug a ditch around it. He put wood on it, and an ox to burn.

"Now bring some water," he said to the men around him.

They brought water — four barrels full. They poured it all on the altar, till the wood and the ox were wet, and the ditch was full.

Then Elijah prayed. He looked up to heaven and said, "O Lord, show us that Thou art truly God, that the people may turn to Thee again."

Then fire came from heaven. The fire burned the ox, the wood, and even the stones. It dried up all the water in the ditch.

And the people said, "The Lord, He is God! He is truly God!"

72

33

A Widow's Oil

(II Kings 4)

There was a great prophet in Israel named Elisha. He did wonderful things to show the power of God.

One day a widow came to Elisha. She was sad, for she had a great trouble. She owed money to a man, and she could not pay it. The man said he would take her boys to be his slaves.

The widow loved her two boys. She did not want them to be slaves. So she went to tell Elisha her trouble.

"Please tell me what to do," she begged.

Elisha said, "Have you something to sell, to earn some money?"

The poor widow shook her head. "No," she said. "I am poor. I have only a little oil in a jar."

Elisha said, "Go to all your neighbors and ask them for jars. Get as many empty jars as you can. Then go into your house. Shut the door. And pour your little bit of oil into the empty jars."

The widow sent her two boys to borrow jars from all the neighbors. They ran, and soon they came back with jars — one, two, three, a long row of jars!

Then the widow closed the door of her house. She told the boys to bring the jars to her, one by one. She poured her little bit of oil into the first jar. She poured until the jar was full! The boys brought another jar, and she poured that one full. Then another, and another — till all the jars were full!

The widow ran to Elisha. She told him how her little bit of oil had filled all the jars.

Elisha said, "Now go. Sell the oil. Then you will have enough money to pay the man. And you will have some left for you and the boys."

The widow soon sold all the oil. She paid the man the money she owed him. And she had some left to buy food for herself and the boys.

So God showed His love and His power through the prophet Elisha.

34

A Letter for God to Read

(*II Kings 19*)

Israel had many kings. Some were good. Some were bad. Hezekiah was one of the good kings. Hezekiah trusted in God and taught the people to serve Him.

But one day a very big army came to Jerusalem, the city where Hezekiah had his palace. It was the army of Assyria. The soldiers put up their tents all around Jerusalem.

The king of Assyria sent a messenger to Hezekiah. He said, "I will take your city. Everything that you have will be mine. You cannot fight against me. You may as well give up."

The people of Jerusalem were afraid of the big army. But Hezekiah said to them, "Do not be afraid. Just trust in God." And he would not give up.

Then the king of Assyria sent a letter to Hezekiah. In the letter he said, "Do you think your God can save Jerusalem? There were other big cities, just as big and strong as Jerusalem. Their gods could not save them. I took all those big cities. And your God cannot save you."

The letter made Hezekiah sad. It was true — the king of Assyria had taken many big cities. His army was very strong.

Hezekiah took the letter and went to the temple. He laid the letter open, for God to read. And Hezekiah prayed.

Hezekiah said, "O Lord, Thou art the only true God. Thou art the God of all the earth. See this letter that the king of Assyria sent me. He says that our God cannot save us. But O Lord, hear us, and save us!"

There was a prophet in Jerusalem at that time. His name was Isaiah. God often spoke to Isaiah.

Now God sent Isaiah to tell Hezekiah the answer to his prayer.

Isaiah said to Hezekiah, "The Lord has heard your prayer. He will drive away the army of Assyria. He will save Jerusalem."

That very night God sent an angel to the army of Assyria. The angel killed many of the soldiers. And the others ran away.

Then the king of Assyria knew that the God of Jerusalem is the only true God. He can save His people.

35

A Book That Told the Truth

(Jeremiah 36)

The people of Israel were God's people. He had chosen them to be His. And He had blessed them with all good things.

But the people of Israel forgot God. They served idols.

Then God sent the prophet Jeremiah to them. God told Jeremiah to write a book. He told Jeremiah just what to write.

Jeremiah wrote all the words of God. He wrote how God would punish Israel for their sin. Jerusalem, the big city, would be broken down. The beautiful Temple and all the beautiful houses would be broken down and burned. The people would be taken away to a strange country.

Last of all he wrote, "But if you are sorry for your sin, if you turn away from sin and serve God now, then these terrible things will not happen."

Somebody took the book to the king. The king sat in his house. And a cozy fire burned in the fireplace.

The man read the book to the king. He read the first page; then he tore it out and threw it in the fire. He read the second page, and he threw that in the fire.

Someone said, "Oh, do not burn the book. It is the prophet's book."

But the king was not afraid. He let the man burn the whole book.

Then the king said, "Now get this Jeremiah. We cannot let him write such horrid books."

But God hid Jeremiah. The king could not find him.

And God said to Jeremiah, "Write the book again. For the terrible things shall surely happen."

Jeremiah did write it again. But the king and the people would not read it or listen to Jeremiah. They went on living in sin.

And then, one day, the king of Babylon came. He had a very big army. He put his army all around Jerusalem. He broke down the walls and took the city. He burned the king's house and the other beautiful houses. He burned the beautiful Temple. He took the king and many of the people to far-away Babylon.

Then the people were sorry. They cried as they walked along the dusty road to Babylon. They looked back and saw their homes on fire. Now they were slaves of the king of Babylon. All that the book said had come true.

36

Daniel in the Lions' Den
(Daniel 6)

Daniel lived in far-away Babylon. He was a young man, and he served God with all his heart. The king trusted him, and made him great in the kingdom of Babylon.

But there were some men who hated Daniel.

These evil men went to the king one day. They said, "O King, you are very great. You should make a law that people must pray to you for thirty days. Tell the people they may not pray to any god. If they want something, they must ask you."

The king thought, "That is fine. That makes me like a god!"

So he made the law, and he wrote his name on it.

Then the evil men went to Daniel's house. They watched Daniel. They looked through the window. And they saw Daniel kneel down to pray. Three times a day Daniel prayed to God.

These evil men hurried back to the king. They said, "O King, you have made a law. Nobody may pray to God. And if anyone does pray to God, he must be thrown into the den of lions."

The king said, "Yes, that is the law I made."

Then the men said, "But Daniel prays! He does not care about the law. Three times a day he prays to God."

The king was sorry to hear that. He did not want to throw Daniel to the lions. But he had to keep the law. So he sent for Daniel.

The king said to Daniel, "Your God can save you." And he let the men throw Daniel into the lion's den.

That night the king could not sleep. He turned and turned on his pillow. He was thinking about Daniel.

Early in the morning the king hurried to the lion's den. He opened the door and called, "Daniel! Daniel! Did your God save you?"

He listened. And yes, he heard Daniel's voice. Daniel said, "Yes, O King! the Lord sent His angels to shut the lions' mouths."

Then they took Daniel out, and they threw the evil men to the lions. And the king made a new law. The law said, "The God of Daniel is the living God. Let everybody fear Him."

37

God Sends His Son

(Luke 2)

Long, long ago, God made a promise. He said He would send a Great King to His people. The King would be greater than any other king ever was. He would give new eyes to the blind. He would make the deaf hear again. He would make sick people well. And He would save His people from their sins.

God's people waited many, many years for God to keep His promise. But at last the time came.

The angel said to the shepherds, "Do not be afraid!"

It was night. All the earth was dark and still. Up in the sky the stars twinkled. And the little city of Bethlehem was asleep.

Around the city of Bethlehem, on the hills, there were flocks of sheep. They were asleep on the green grass.

But near the sheep were the shepherds. They were wide awake. They were keeping watch over their flocks by night. They sat together and talked together, softly, in the dark.

Suddenly the shepherds saw a bright light in the sky. It was like the light of the sun. It shone around the shepherds, and they were afraid.

Then they saw an angel, standing in the light.

The angel said to the shepherds, "Do not be afraid. I have good news for you. The Saviour, Christ the Lord, is born today in Bethlehem! You may go see Him. You will find Him in a manger, wrapped in swaddling clothes."

Then the sky was full of bright angels. The angels sang, "Glory to God! Glory to God in the highest! Peace on earth. Good will to men!"

The shepherds listened and listened. After a while the angels went back to heaven. The light faded away.

The the shepherds said, "Let's go to Bethlehem and see the Baby!"

They hurried down the dark hill. They hunted till they found the Baby in a stable. Mary, the Baby's mother, was there. And Joseph, her husband, was there. And the Baby lay in a manger.

The shepherds kneeled down by the manger, to worship Him. This Baby was Jesus Christ, the Lord, the Great King.

The shepherds went back to their sheep, praising God. For the Great King, promised so long ago, had come at last!

38

God Makes Two Old People Happy

(Luke 2:21-41)

In Jerusalem there once were two old people who loved God very much. One was an old man. His name was Simeon. The other was an old lady. Her name was Anna.

Simeon and Anna knew about God's promise — that some day He would send a Great King to save His people. And they were hoping to see that Great King before they died.

One day the Holy Spirit spoke to Simeon. God told Simeon that he would surely see the Great King before he died. So Simeon waited.

And after a while the Holy Spirit spoke to Simeon again. He told Simeon to go to the Temple.

Simeon went. When he came to the Temple, he saw a man and a lady there, with a baby. It was Joseph and Mary, with Baby Jesus! And the Holy Spirit in Simeon's heart told Simeon that this Baby was the Great King, the Saviour.

Then Simeon went to see the Baby. He took the Baby in his arms, and looked at Him. This Baby was the King! And Simeon held Him!

Simeon looked up to heaven and said, "O Lord, now I have seen the Saviour. Now I am ready to die."

He told Joseph and Mary that wonderful things would happen to this Baby. And he blessed Joseph and Mary.

Anna was in the Temple, too. She came there every day, to worship God. When Anna saw Simeon hold the Baby, she came to see Him. And the Holy Spirit in her heart told her that this was the Great Saviour King.

Then Anna was happy, too. She praised God.

Joseph and Mary went back home with the Baby. But Simeon and Anna stayed in the Temple. They praised God all day long. When other people came to the Temple, they told them about the Baby Jesus. For at last the Saviour had come.

39

Jesus' Star

(*Matthew 2:1-12*)

When Jesus was born in Bethlehem, a beautiful bright star shone in the sky.

Far away, many miles from Bethlehem, some wise men saw the star. They said, "Surely this new star means that there is a new king! Such a bright star must mean a very great king!"

These wise men wanted to see the new king. They took gifts for the king — gold and frankincense and myrrh. And they rode away on their camels, to Jerusalem.

There was a king in Jerusalem named Herod. And the wise men went to his palace. They said to king Herod, "Where is the new king? We saw his star in the east."

King Herod shook his head. He did not know anything at all about a new king.

But Herod did know that, long ago, God had promised to send a Great King to Israel. So he called the teachers of the Jews. He asked them where the Great King should be born.

They said, "In Bethlehem."

Herod told the wise men. And he said, "If you find the king, come and tell me. I want to worship Him, too."

The wise men hurried away, toward Bethlehem.

When night came, and the stars began to twinkle, they saw the big bright star again! How happy they were then! The star moved on, and the wise men followed it. The star led them to Bethlehem, and shone on a house there.

The wise men knocked at the door — and in that house they found the Baby Jesus, with Mary and Joseph.

The wise men fell down on their knees by the Baby. They gave Him their gifts — gold and frankincense and myrrh. And they thanked God for the wonderful star that led them to Jesus, the Great King.

But they did not go back to Herod. An angel came to tell them, in a dream, to go back another way. Herod was a wicked man. He would kill the new King, if he could.

40

Jesus in His Father's House

(*Luke 2:41-50*)

Jesus grew up in Nazareth, a little city far from Jerusalem. He grew up like other boys and girls. He learned to read and write. He played games. He helped Joseph and Mary.

But Jesus was different from other boys. He had a pure and sinless heart. He was never selfish or naughty or rude. For Jesus was the Son of God.

Once every year, Joseph and Mary went to Jerusalem. They went to the Temple there, to worship God. When Jesus was twelve years old, they took Him along.

That was a happy time. Very many people went to Jerusalem. They walked along together. They ate their lunches by the roadside. They slept under the stars at night.

When at last they came near Jerusalem, they could see the towers of the beautiful Temple.

Jesus saw many new things in Jerusalem. But the Temple was best of all. That was His Father's House.

At last it was time to go home again. The older people walked together, talking about all they had seen. The children ran and played. All day long they walked on and on. When evening came, they were going to sleep under the stars.

Mary and Joseph called Jesus to come with them. But He did not come. Then they looked for Him, but they could not find Him. They asked, and nobody knew where He was.

Joseph and Mary said, "He is lost! We must go back and find Him."

They hurried back to Jerusalem. They walked up and down the streets of Jerusalem. They looked everywhere. But they could not find Jesus.

At last they went to the Temple — and there He was!

Jesus was talking with some big men. They asked Him questions, and He answered them. They talked about God.

Joseph and Mary listened. How could Jesus talk with these wise men? He was only a boy!

But they said to Him, "Son, we have hunted and hunted for you. We came all the way back. We were worried."

Jesus said, "Why did you worry? Don't you know that I must do my Father's work?"

But Jesus went home with Mary and Joseph, to Nazareth. He was the Son of God, but He obeyed Mary and Joseph.

85

41
A Voice From Heaven
(*Matthew 3:13-17; Mark 1:1-8; Luke 3:21, 22*)

By the river Jordan there lived a strange man. He lived alone in the wilderness. He lived close to God, and talked with God. And God gave him a message for the people.

When people came to the wilderness to hear this man preach, he told them they must be sorry for their sins. And he baptized them in the river. So he was called John the Baptist.

Many people said, "Who is this John? Is he a prophet?"

But John said, "I came to make the way ready for another. He is coming. And He is greater than I. He will baptize you with the Holy Spirit."

Even John did not know who this Great Someone was.

But one day God said to John, "The Spirit of God will come down from heaven, like a dove. It will rest on the head of a man. That man is the Son of God."

Every day John preached by the river. He baptized the people who were sorry for their sins.

And then, one day, Jesus came to John. Jesus was a young man now. He came to John to be baptized.

John and Jesus went down into the river together. John baptized Jesus.

And when they came out of the water, John saw the heavens open. He saw the Holy Spirit, like a dove, come down upon Jesus' head. And he heard a voice from heaven. The voice said, "This is my beloved Son. Hear Him!"

Then John knew that Jesus is the Son of God.

After that, when John saw Jesus again, He pointed to Him and said, "See the Lamb of God! He takes away the sin of the world!"

42

Two Men Visit Jesus

(*John 1:35-43*)

One day John the Baptist stood by the river Jordan with two men. They were talking together. After a while they saw Jesus walking down the path by the river.

John said to the two men, "See! There is the Lamb of God!"

Then the two men began to follow Jesus.

Jesus turned around. He saw the two men following Him.

Jesus said, "What are you looking for?"

The two men said, "Master, where do you live?"

Jesus said to them, "Come and see where I live."

So the two men went along with Jesus and they visited with Jesus all that day.

What a wonderful visit that was! Jesus talked with them. He told them about the Kingdom of God. He told them wonderful things. Then they were sure that Jesus must be the Christ, the Great King.

When the sun set, they said goodbye to Jesus. They went home.

One of the two men was Andrew. He hurried home to tell his brother Simon about Jesus.

Then Simon wanted to see Jesus, too. So the next day Andrew and Simon went together.

Jesus saw Andrew and Simon come.

Jesus said to Simon, "You are Simon. But after this your name shall be Peter."

Simon was surprised. How could Jesus know his name?

Jesus talked to Simon and Andrew for a long time. Then Simon, too, knew that Jesus must be the Christ, the Son of God.

43
Jesus Calls His Disciples
(Matthew 4:18-22; Mark 1:16-20; John 1:43-51)

One day when Jesus was walking down the road, He saw a man named Philip. Jesus said to Philip, "Follow me!"

Philip looked at Jesus. Philip did not ask, "Why must I follow you?" He just put his work away. He followed Jesus.

Philip had a friend named Nathaniel. Philip told Nathaniel about Jesus. Then Nathaniel came to Jesus. He followed Jesus, too.

After a while, Jesus went to the Sea of Galilee. Simon and Andrew were in a little boat, out on the water. They were fishing.

Jesus stood on the shore. Jesus called to them, "Follow me, and I will make you fishers of men!"

Then Simon and Andrew rowed the little boat to shore. They pulled the boat up on shore. And they went to Jesus.

There was another little boat near the shore. Three men were in it — Zebedee, and his two sons, James and John.

Jesus called to James and John. They looked up and saw Him on the shore.

Jesus said to them, "Come and follow me!"

James and John put their nets down. They said good-bye to Zebedee, their father. And they went to follow Jesus.

Jesus found more men. He called them. And they followed Him. These men were Jesus' disciples. After a while Jesus had twelve disciples.

The twelve disciples followed Jesus wherever He went. Jesus told them about God, and about all the wonders of the Kingdom of God.

44

A Visit at Night

(*John 3:1-21*)

It was night. Jesus had been very busy all day. He had made many sick people well. He had made blind men to see. He had told all of them about God. Now He was tired, and He was resting, alone, on a roof-top.

Then Jesus heard a voice. A man asked if he could come up. He wanted to talk with Jesus. He came at night, to talk with Jesus alone.

This man's name was Nicodemus. He was a teacher of the Jews.

Nicodemus said to Jesus, "We know that you surely came from God. You do such wonderful things! You make sick people well; you heal the blind; you could not do such wonderful things if you did not come from God."

Jesus said to Nicodemus, "If you want to see the Kingdom of God, you must be born again."

But Nicodemus said, "How can that be? How can a grown-up man be born again? How can he become a child again?"

Jesus said, "You must be born of the Holy Spirit. You must become a child of God."

Nicodemus did not know how to become a child of God. He asked Jesus many questions. Jesus said to him, "Do you know the story of the serpent in the desert?"

Yes, Nicodemus knew the story: Long, long ago the people of Israel were in a desert. There they sinned against God. They grumbled and complained. Then God sent serpents. The serpents bit many people, so that many died. But when the people cried to God, He heard them. He told Moses to make a serpent of shin-

Nicodemus came at night,
to talk with Jesus alone.

91

ing brass, to put it on a pole, and to set it up high. Anybody who looked at the shining serpent was made well.

Jesus said, "The Son of man must be lifted up like the serpent. Anyone who believes on Him will live forever.

"For God so loved the world that He gave His only begotten Son, that whosoever believeth on Him should not perish, but have everlasting life."

Jesus and Nicodemus talked a long time. Nicodemus learned that he must believe on Jesus. Only those who believe on Jesus are truly children of God.

Nicodemus went home. He thought and thought about the words of Jesus. After a while he believed on Jesus. He believed that Jesus is the Son of God, the Saviour.

45

Four Fishermen

(*Luke 5:1-11*)

There is a beautiful lake in the land of Palestine. It is the Sea of Galilee.

One day four men went fishing on the Sea of Galilee. Peter and Andrew went in one little boat. James and John went in another little boat.

The four fishermen used nets. They would throw the nets into the water. Then they would slowly pull the nets out. Sometimes they caught fish this way. But that day they did not catch any.

All night long the four fishermen fished. But they did not catch even one fish.

In the morning they gave up. They rowed to shore. They pulled the boats up on the sand. They took their nets into the water to wash them.

But just then a man came along. Many people were with that man. It was Jesus.

Jesus said to Peter, "Push the boat into the water a little way."

Peter did. And Jesus sat down in the boat. Now all the people could sit on shore and see Jesus. He talked to them from the boat.

Jesus told them about God. And there was so much to tell! The people liked to listen to Jesus.

At last Jesus finished talking, and the people went away. Then Jesus said to Peter, "Let us go far out now, into deep water, and go fishing."

Peter said, "We were out fishing all night. We did not catch even one fish. But if you say so, we will try again."

So Peter and Andrew rowed the little boat out into deep water. There they let the net down. Then they pulled it up. And this time it was full of fishes! The net was so full that it began to tear.

Peter and Andrew could not pull it up alone. They called to James and John, on shore. "Come and help us!"

James and John quickly pushed their little boat into the water. They rowed as fast as they could. And all together they pulled up the net. They put the fish into the boats until both boats were full.

Then Peter knew Jesus was not only a man. And Peter was afraid. He fell down on his knees by Jesus. "O Lord," he said, "I am a sinful man!"

But Jesus said to Peter, "Do not be afraid. After this you shall catch men."

They rowed to shore. They pulled the boats up on the sand. And they left the boats there, fish and all. Other people could have the fish. Peter and Andrew and James and John went with Jesus. They followed Him and became His disciples.

46

Down Through the Roof

(Mark 2:1-13; Luke 5:18-27)

In the city of Capernaum there was a very sick man. He lay on his bed all the time. He could not get up and walk.

This sick man heard about Jesus. He heard that Jesus made sick people well. But he could not get up and go to Jesus.

Then, one day, four friends came to see the sick man. They said to him, "Jesus is in our city. We will carry you to Him!"

Each took hold of a corner of the sick man's bed. They carried him, bed and all, down the street. They carried him straight to the house where Jesus was.

But when they came to the house, they found people standing all around it. There was a big crowd. The four men with the bed could not even get near the door.

"Now what shall we do?" they said.

The poor sick man was very sorry. It seemed they would not get to Jesus after all. They could not get through the crowd.

But one man said, "The house is small. We can go upon the roof. We can let the bed down right through the roof, right in front of Jesus."

94

That was a good plan.

The roof was flat. And there were steps to go up. People of that country often sit upon their roofs.

So the four men went up, carrying the bed and the sick man. They laid the bed down on the roof. Then they made a hole. When they looked down, they saw Jesus.

Next they tied a rope on each corner of the bed. They held the four ropes. They carefully let the bed down, down, right in front of Jesus.

The people down there looked up in surprise. What was this? A bed coming down through the roof!

But Jesus was not surprised.

Jesus looked at the sick man and He said, "Your sins are forgiven."

The people were surprised again. Only God can forgive sins. They did not know that Jesus is the Son of God.

Then Jesus said to the sick man, "You may get up. Pick up your bed. You can walk."

The sick man sat up. Then he stood up. And he knew he was well again!

How happy he was! He said "Thank you!" to Jesus again and again.

Then he rolled up his bed and took it under his arm. He went away. His face was all smiles and his eyes were shining. He was well. He could walk. He could even run.

The people in the house praised God. They said, "We never saw such wonderful things before."

47
Jesus Turns Tears to Smiles
(*Luke 7:11-18*)

Jesus went from city to city. In every city He did good. He healed the sick. He made the blind to see. He made the deaf to hear.

The people loved Jesus. They followed Him. They listened when He told them about the Kingdom of God.

One day Jesus walked along the road to Nain. Nain was a little city. Jesus' disciples, and many other people, were with Him.

When they came near the city, they saw a crowd of people come out of the city gate. These people walked slowly. They were sad. It was a funeral.

Some men carried a coffin. On the coffin lay a young man. His mother was walking beside the coffin. She was weeping. She was a widow, and this young man was her only son. Her friends were weeping, too.

Jesus felt sorry for the poor widow. When He came near the funeral, he said to the widow, "Do not weep."

Then He put out His hand and touched the coffin. The men who carried the coffin stopped. They stood still. They wondered what Jesus would do.

Jesus looked at the young man. He lay there on the coffin so still and cold. And Jesus said, "Young man, I say to thee, arise!"

The young man was dead. But he heard the voice of Jesus. He sat up. He was alive. He looked around. He looked at Jesus, the wonderful Jesus. And he looked at his mother.

His mother was not weeping now. Her tears were all gone. They were turned to smiles. And all the people were happy with her.

The people said, "This Jesus is a great prophet! Surely God sent Him. For only God can make a dead man alive!"

48

A Foolish Rich Man

(*Luke 12:16-20*)

Sometimes Jesus told stories to the people. One day He told them this story:

Once upon a time there was a rich man. He had a very big farm. He had very big barns on his farm. Every year he cut the wheat and hay and corn on his farm, and put it all into his barns.

One summer he had very much wheat and hay and corn. He put it into his barns till they were full. And then he had a great deal left. He had never been so rich before.

The rich man said to himself, "What shall I do with all the wheat and hay and corn? I shall build more barns, and bigger barns. Then I can put all my wheat and hay and corn into my barns, and keep it."

The rich man thought how fine it would be to have so much. He said to himself, "When my barns are all full, I shall be happy. I will not have to work. I can eat and drink and be happy all day long. I will be happy for many, many years."

But in the night God came to the rich man. God said to the rich man, "How foolish you are! Tonight I shall take your soul away. You shall die. Then who will have your wheat and hay and corn?"

So the foolish man died. God took his soul away in the night.

And then he was not rich at all. For he did not have a home in heaven.

He was a very foolish rich man.

A really rich man is one who is rich in God. He has a home in heaven.

49

A Lesson From Lilies and Birds

(Luke 12:22-32)

It was a beautiful spring day. Jesus sat down on a hillside. And the people sat around Him to hear Him talk. The hill was green with grass. There were many pretty flowers, too. And up in the blue sky the birds were flying.

Jesus said, "See the birds. They do not put food away into barns. They do not worry. God takes care of them. God feeds them."

Then Jesus stood and pointed to the lilies in the grass.

He said, "Look at the lilies. See how they grow. The lily petals are more beautiful than any silk or satin. Even Solomon, the rich king, did not have clothes as pretty as the petals of a lily.

"But the lilies do not work hard to make their pretty petals. And they do not worry about tomorrow. They just grow. God gave them their pretty petals."

The people looked up at the birds. They looked down at the pretty lilies in the grass.

Jesus said, "Your Father in heaven takes care of them. And you are worth much more than the birds and the lilies. Surely He will take care of you. He knows what you need. You must love Him best of all, and He will take care of you."

For the little birds in the sky, and the lilies in the grass, tell us that God cares for us.

Jesus taught the people lessons from the lilies and the birds.

50

Jesus Raises a Little Girl

(Matthew 9:18-27; Mark 5:21-43; Luke 8:41-56)

There was a rich man named Jairus. He had a little girl twelve years old.

One day this little girl became sick. Jairus called the doctor, but the doctor could not help her. The little girl's sickness grew worse and worse.

Then someone told Jairus that Jesus was coming to the city.

Jairus knew that Jesus could heal the sick. Quickly he hurried to find Jesus.

Jesus was walking up the street, in a crowd of people. But these people knew Jairus. They let him through to Jesus.

Jairus was a rich man, but he fell down on his knees before Jesus. He said to Jesus, "Please come to my house. My little girl is very sick. She is about to die."

Jesus said, "I will come."

But Jesus did not hurry. There was such a big crowd, He could not hurry. Jairus could hardly wait. He was afraid the little girl would die.

Then a sick woman came through the crowd. She came behind Jesus, and touched His robe. And she was well. Jesus stopped to talk with her. And she was very happy. But Jairus wanted Jesus to hurry.

While Jesus talked with the woman, a man came running down the street. He came straight to Jairus. He said, "Don't bother the Master. It is too late. Your little girl is dead."

Too late. Sadly Jairus turned to go home. There was no use waiting for Jesus now.

But Jesus stopped Jairus. He said, "Do not be afraid. Only believe."

Then the crowd let Jesus through. He went home with Jairus.

In Jairus' house there were many people. All of them were weeping aloud. They said, "The little girl is dead! She is dead!"

Jesus told them not to weep. He said, "She is asleep."

Then some of them laughed. They said, "But no, she is dead."

All the people wanted to go with Jesus to see the little girl on her bed. But Jesus would not let them go. He took just three of His disciples—Peter, James, and John. And He took the mother and father of the little girl. Then He went into the room where the little girl lay on her bed.

She lay very still and cold. She was dead.

Jesus took hold of her little cold hand. He held it in His warm hand. And He said, "Little girl, get up!"

Then the little girl's spirit came back. She opened her eyes. She sat up and looked around — at her mother and father, and at Jesus. She was alive, and she was well.

The mother took the little girl in her arms and held her close. A minute ago she was dead! Now she was alive and well.

Jesus told them to give her something to eat. Then He went away.

All the people in the house, and the big crowd out-doors, heard how Jesus made the little girl alive. They said, "What a wonderful man this Jesus is!"

51

A Little Boy's Lunch Grows Big

(*Matthew 14:13-22; Mark 6:30-45; John 6:1-14*)

One day Jesus was tired. He said to His disciples, "Let us go away, to a quiet place. Then we can rest a while."

They went into the little boat. They rowed away on the blue lake.

But the people could not bear to see Jesus go away. They wanted to be with Him all the time. So they said, "We can follow Him. We can walk along the shore, and watch where the boat goes."

And they did. They walked along the shore of the big blue lake. Some were sick, and some were old. Some carried little babies. There were little children and big children. They all walked along the shore. They wanted to be with Jesus.

Most of them did not even stop to take a lunch along. But one little boy did take a lunch. He had five little loaves of bread, like biscuits, and two little fish.

While they walked along the shore, they watched the little boat. They saw just where it was going. When it came to the quiet place, they were waiting for it!

Jesus loved the people, and He felt sorry for them. So He sat down on the green hill and began telling them about God once more. He told them how they must love Him and trust Him. And He healed all the sick.

But after a while the sun began to go down. Soon it would be supper time.

The disciples said to Jesus, "The people should go home now. It is time to eat."

Jesus said, "Why don't you give them something to eat?"

The disciples looked at the big crowd. There were hundreds and hundreds of people. They said to Jesus, "Why, where could we buy bread for so many? And we have not enough money to buy bread."

Then Andrew saw the little boy who had a lunch. He called the little boy. The little boy was glad to give his lunch to Jesus. But five little loaves and two little fishes — one hungry boy could eat that much!

"What is such a little bit for so many people!" said Andrew.

Jesus said, "Tell the people to sit down."

So the disciples told all the people to sit down on the grass.

Then Jesus took the little boy's bread. He looked up to heaven. He thanked God for the food. And He broke the little loaves of bread in pieces. He gave the pieces to the disciples. And they passed the bread to the people.

They came back to Jesus for more, and more, and more. They passed bread to the people till all had enough.

Jesus broke the fish into pieces, too. And the disciples passed the pieces of fish to the people. All the people had enough to eat.

There were more than five thousand people. But the five little loaves of bread, and the two little fish, were enough for all. There were even pieces left. The disciples picked up twelve little baskets full.

For Jesus had made the little boy's lunch grow big — big enough for hundreds and hundreds of people.

52

Jesus Walks on the Waves

(*Matthew 14:22-33; Mark 6:45-52; John 6:16-22*)

The sun was setting. Soon it would be dark. But the people on the hill by the lake did not want to go home. They wanted to stay there, with Jesus.

Then Jesus said to the disciples, "You get into the boat, and row away. I will send the people home."

The disciples obeyed Jesus. They rowed the little boat away on the big lake.

Jesus talked with the people a little longer. He sent them away. And at last He was alone.

When Jesus was alone on the green hill, He kneeled down to pray. He liked to be alone with God. For a long time He kneeled there, talking with God.

When He stood up, it was dark. He looked away across the lake, across the dark water. And He saw the disciples in the little boat, out on the lake. For Jesus can see through the dark.

The lake was stormy. A rough wind made big waves. Jesus saw the little boat rock on the big waves. The wind was so rough that the disciples could not row the boat.

Then Jesus went to the water. And He walked right out on the water, toward the little boat. He did not sink down into the water. He walked on the tops of the waves.

Farther and farther out on the stormy lake Jesus walked. When He came near the little boat, the disciples saw Him.

But the disciples did not know that it was Jesus. They saw something white in the dark. They saw it come toward the boat. And they were afraid.

Then Jesus called to them, "Do not be afraid. It is I!"

They knew Jesus' voice. But how could Jesus be there, on the water?

Peter said, "Lord, is it really you? Then tell me to come to you, on the water!"

Jesus said to Peter, "Come!"

Peter quickly climbed out of the boat. He went to Jesus. He walked on the tops of the waves, just as Jesus did!

But suddenly Peter saw a big wave come. And he was afraid. Then he began to sink down into the cold dark water.

Peter cried out, "Lord, help me!"

Jesus quickly put out His hand. He took hold of Peter and held him up.

Jesus said to Peter, "Why were you afraid?"

Peter did not need to be afraid, with Jesus so near.

Then they walked to the boat together.

When they were in the boat, the wind stopped. And the disciples fell down at Jesus' feet. They said, "Thou art the Son of God."

53

Three Crosses on a Hill

(*Matthew 27:31-39; Mark 15:20-28; Luke 23:26-34*)

Early one morning there were soldiers marching through the streets of Jerusalem. They marched out of the city, out to the country.

They did not march fast. Between the soldiers was a man who carried a big heavy cross. He could not go fast.

People heard the soldiers march. They came running to see. They saw the man with the cross. And it was Jesus!

Yes, the soldiers were taking Jesus away. They were going to nail Him to the cross.

There were wicked men who hated Jesus. They wanted Him to die. They told the governor that He must be crucified. And the governor gave Jesus to the soldiers. Now they were taking Him away, up the hill.

But surely Jesus could get away from the soldiers? He was the Son of God. He healed all kinds of sicknesses. He raised people from the dead. Even the wind and the waves obeyed Him. Surely He could make the soldiers let Him go. Yes, He could. Or He could ask God for angels to help Him.

But Jesus did not want to do that. Jesus wanted to go up the hill to be crucified. He came down to earth to die upon the cross. He came to die for sinners like you and me.

The people followed the soldiers up the hill. The cross was very heavy. Jesus could hardly carry it. So the soldiers made a man named Simon help Him.

At last they were on the top of the hill. Simon laid the cross on the ground. The soldiers laid Jesus on the cross. And they nailed Him to the cross. They put nails through His hands and through His feet.

The nails hurt Jesus' hands and feet. But Jesus prayed for the soldiers. He said, "Father, forgive them, for they know not what they do."

The soldiers did not know that Jesus is the Son of God. They did not know that He is the Great King sent by God.

The soldiers dug a hole in the ground. They set the cross in the hole. And all the people could see Jesus, hanging there on the cross.

There were three crosses on the hill. Two other men were crucified with Jesus. They were robbers.

At noon, when the sun was high, the sky became very dark. God took the light away, because His Son was on the cross.

Out of the darkness Jesus cried, "It is finished!"

His work was done. He had paid for our sins. Then He gave His soul to God and He died.

His friends came to bury Him. They were very sad. They put Him in a new grave in Joseph's garden. They rolled a big stone in front of the grave. Then it was night. They went sadly home.

54

The Resurrection

(*Matthew 28:1-9; Mark 16:1-12; Luke 24:1-12; John 20:11-19*)

It was very quiet in Joseph's garden. The big moon shone bright and made a soft light around Jesus' grave.

Soldiers were sitting in the moonlight. They were soldiers sent to watch over Jesus' grave.

But suddenly the soldiers felt the ground shake. And a bright light, like lightning, flashed from the sky. The bright light came down to earth, came straight to the garden, came straight to the grave of Jesus. It was an angel!

The soldiers were afraid. They fell down on their faces. And when they dared to look up, they saw that the grave was open. The stone was rolled away. And the angel was sitting on the stone.

Then the soldiers jumped up and ran away.

And all was quiet in the garden again.

The big moon went down in the west. The bright sun came up in the east. It was Sunday morning.

Some people came walking up the hill. They were coming toward the grave. They were women. One was Mary Magdalene, who loved Jesus very much. The women talked together softly.

"There is a big stone in front of the grave," said one. "Who will roll it away for us?"

But then they looked — and the stone was rolled away!

Mary Magdalene cried, "Oh, oh! Somebody has stolen the body of Jesus!"

And she turned around to run back to Jerusalem. She ran to tell the disciples.

The other women went close to the grave. And there they saw the shining angel. His face was like lightning. They were afraid.

But the angel said to them, "Do not be afraid. I know you are looking for Jesus. He is not here. He is risen. He is alive! Go tell the disciples that He is risen!"

The women looked at each other. Could it be true? Could it really be true? An angel said so!

Then they ran back to Jerusalem, to tell the disciples.

But Mary Magdalene came back to the garden alone. She looked everywhere to find the body of Jesus. But she could not find it. At last she sat down and wept.

After a while Mary saw a man standing near by. The man said to her, "Why are you weeping?"

Mary said, "They have taken my Lord away! Did you take Him? Please tell me where you put Him!"

The man looked at her and said, "Mary!"

Then Mary saw that it was Jesus.

Mary fell at Jesus' feet. "My Master! My Master!" she said.

Jesus said, "Now go tell my disciples."

So once again Mary ran to Jerusalem. This time she had the best news of all. "Jesus is alive! He is risen! I saw Him!"

Mary ran to tell the disciples,
"I have seen Jesus. He is alive!"

55

Two Men Walk With Jesus

(Luke 24:13-32)

It was afternoon, on Easter day. Two disciples went for a walk to Emmaus. On the way, they talked and talked. They talked about Jesus.

After a while a strange man came to walk with them. The man said, "What are you talking about?"

They said, "Oh, we are talking about all the wonderful things that have happened."

The strange man said, "What wonderful things?"

The disciples said, "Don't you know? Didn't you hear about Jesus? We thought He was a great prophet. We thought He would be our king. But the chief priests took Him, and He died on the cross. We thought surely He would be the Saviour."

And they had more to tell. They said, "This morning some friends went to His grave. They came running back. They said the grave was empty. They said they saw angels by the grave, and the angels said Jesus is alive."

Then the strange man said, "Don't you understand? The Saviour had to die on the cross. Long, long ago, the prophets said that He would come, and that He would die on the cross, and that He would live again."

The strange man told them all about the prophets of long, long ago. The disciples listened. They thought, "What a wonderful man this strange man is!"

After a while they came to Emmaus. The disciples stopped at their house.

The strange man was going to walk on. But the disciples said, "Come in and eat supper with us."

They all went into the house. All three sat down to eat supper.

Then the strange man took bread. He looked up to heaven and asked God to bless the bread. And He broke a piece for each of the two disciples.

When they saw the man break the bread, they suddenly knew who it was. It was Jesus!

But at that very moment Jesus was gone.

The two disciples looked at each other with shining eyes. They said, "No wonder we thought He was a wonderful Man!"

56

Jesus Comes Through a Closed Door

(*Luke 24:33-48; John 20:19, 20*)

The two disciples in Emmaus could not eat their supper. They were too happy to eat. They had seen Jesus!

They said to each other, "We must tell the other disciples! Let us go back to Jerusalem right now!"

Jerusalem was far away, and night was coming. But they went just the same. They could not wait to tell the good news.

They hurried to the house of the disciples in Jerusalem. They knocked at the door.

Somebody opened the door and said, "Jesus is alive! Peter saw Him!"

"Oh!" said the men from Emmaus, "we saw Him, too!"

Then they closed the door tight, and began to talk. They told how Jesus walked with them and talked with them. They told how He broke the bread.

And then — there Jesus was, right in the room. He did not open the door. He just stood there, in the middle of the room. All the disciples looked at Him with big wondering eyes.

Jesus said, "Peace be unto you."

But they were afraid. They could not believe that it was Jesus.

Jesus said, "Do not be afraid. It is really I. Look at my hands, and look at my feet."

He showed them His hands and His feet. They saw the holes of the big nails. But still they could not believe that Jesus was alive.

Jesus said, "Have you something here to eat?"

Yes, they had a piece of fish. They gave it to Jesus, and He ate it. Then they knew that He was really alive.

Jesus talked with them a long time. He told them that He had to die on the cross. He told them that He took our sins to the cross.

Then Jesus went away again.

But the disciples were very happy. Now they were sure. They knew Jesus was alive. They knew He was the Saviour, the Son of God.

But Thomas was not there.

57

Jesus Comes to the Disciples Again

(*John 20:26-31*)

When Jesus was gone, the disciples talked and talked. How wonderful, that Jesus died on the cross, and then lived again!

After a while Thomas came in.

The disciples said to Thomas, "We have seen Jesus! He is alive!"

Thomas said, "That cannot be. I do not believe it."

They told Thomas all about it. Peter had seen Jesus. Mary Magdalene had seen Jesus. Jesus walked to Emmaus. And Jesus even came into the room, when the door was shut tight.

But Thomas shook his head.

Thomas said, "I will not believe it, unless I put my finger in the nail holes, and put my hand in the spear hole in His side."

A whole week went by. Nobody saw Jesus. Thomas was sure that Jesus was dead.

It was Sunday night again. All the disciples were in the room again. Thomas was there, too.

They talked about Jesus. The door was closed tight. And suddenly Jesus was there, in the middle of the room.

Jesus said, "Peace be unto you."

Then Jesus looked at Thomas.

Jesus said, "Look at my hands. Come put your finger in the nail holes. Put your hand in my side. And believe."

But Thomas did not need to put his finger in the nail holes. He knew it was Jesus. He believed.

Thomas said, "My Lord and my God!" He knew Jesus was the Son of God, the Saviour.

Then Jesus said, "You see Me, and you believe. Many people will not see Me, but they will believe. Blessed are those who will not see Me, and yet believe."

That means you and me. We do not see Jesus. But if we do believe that He is the Son of God, our Saviour, we are truly blessed.

58

A Meeting by the Lake

(John 21:1-15)

One day Peter and John and some other disciples went to the lake — to the Sea of Galilee. They went fishing in their little boat. They had not seen Jesus for a long time.

They put their net down into the water, and they pulled it up again. But there was not one fish in the net.

They tried again and again. All night long, under the stars, they tried. But they did not catch one fish.

At last the stars faded away. The dark sky turned rosy pink. The sun rose. It shone on the water and on the shore.

Then the disciples saw a man standing on the shore.

The man called to them, "Did you catch any fish? Have you some to eat?"

The disciples called back, "No!"

The man said, "Put the net down on the other side of the boat."

The disciples did that. They put the net down. And when they pulled it up, it was full of fishes.

John whispered to Peter, "It is Jesus!"

Then Peter jumped into the water and waded to shore. He wanted to get to Jesus as quickly as possible.

The other disciples rowed the boat, and pulled the net along. Peter helped them pull the net up on shore. They took out the fishes. And they counted one hundred and fifty-three.

On the shore they saw a little fire. And on the fire some fish were frying. There was bread, too. Jesus had breakfast ready for the disciples. So they ate together, and talked with Jesus, like they used to do.

Not many days after that, it was time for Jesus to go to heaven. He took the disciples up on a little hill, near Jerusalem. There He talked with them. He told them they must go into all the world to tell the people the gospel story. They must tell about Jesus, the Saviour, who died and rose again.

He said to them, "The Holy Spirit will come. He will make you strong. He will tell you where to go and what to do."

Then Jesus lifted up His hands over the heads of His disciples. He blessed them.

116

And while He blessed them, He was lifted up. He was lifted up from the ground. Slowly He went higher and higher, up to the sky. When He was high, a cloud came to hide Him.

The disciples looked and looked up at the sky. Jesus was gone!

Then suddenly two men stood beside the disciples. They were dressed in white. They were angels. They said, "Why do you look up to heaven so? Jesus will come again. He will come to earth again, with the clouds." Then the disciples went back to Jerusalem.

59

The Man by the Temple Gate
(*Acts 3*)

There was a lame man in Jerusalem. He could not walk. When he was a little boy, his feet did not grow strong. Now he was a man, and still he could not walk.

Every day some friends brought the lame man to the Temple. They set him by the Temple door. He sat there till they came to get him again.

When the people came to the Temple, the lame man would put out his hand. Many kind people gave him money.

One day, early in the morning, Peter and John came to the Temple. They saw the lame man, and they stopped by him.

Peter said, "Look at us."

The lame man looked at Peter and John. He thought they would give him money.

But Peter said, "I have no silver and no gold. But I have something else to give you."

Then Peter took hold of the man's hand. Peter said, "In the name of Jesus Christ, stand up and walk!"

All at once the lame man felt his feet grow strong. He jumped up. He could walk! And he could jump!

There were many people in the Temple. They saw a man come running and skipping into the Temple. They looked at him, and they said, "That is the lame man. He used to sit by the Temple gate!"

Then they looked at Peter and John. How could this lame man walk?

Peter said, "Do not look at us so. We did not make this man walk. It was Jesus who made him strong and well."

Then Peter told them about Jesus, the Son of God. Peter told how Jesus died on the cross for our sins, how He arose from the grave, and how He went to heaven.

Many people heard it, and many believed on Jesus.

But the enemies of Jesus said to Peter and John, "You must not talk about this Jesus any more." And they put Peter and the other disciples in prison.

But Peter and John said, "God has told us to preach Jesus everywhere. We must obey Him."

When they came out of prison, they went to the Temple to preach about Jesus again. And many believed.

Peter and John and the other disciples were not afraid. The Holy Spirit was in their hearts. The Holy Spirit made them strong and brave.

60

Jesus Calls Saul

(*Acts 9:1-10; 22:4-17; 26:9-19*)

In Jerusalem there was a young man named Saul. He wanted to serve God with all his heart. But he did not believe in Jesus. He hated Jesus. And he tried to put all Christians in prison.

A light brighter than the sun blinded Saul, and he was afraid.

One day Saul went to the big city of Damascus. He was going to put the Damascus Christians in prison. He rode away with a band of men.

But as they rode along in the bright sunshine, they suddenly saw another light, brighter than the sun. This bright light shone on Saul and his men. They were all afraid. They fell down, to hide their faces from the light.

Then Saul heard a voice. The voice called to him, "Saul! Saul! Why do you persecute Me?"

Saul did not know who was talking. He said, "Who are you, Lord?"

The voice said, "I am Jesus!"

That voice came from heaven. Jesus, up in heaven, was calling Saul. Now Saul knew that Jesus is the Son of God.

Then Saul was afraid. He said, "Lord, what must I do?"

Jesus said, "Go to Damascus. I will show you what you must do."

Saul stood up. But he could not see. They led him to Damascus. And there Saul began to pray.

Then God sent a man to him. Ananias came to Saul. He put his hands on Saul's head, and he said, "Brother Saul, Jesus sent me to you."

Then Saul's eyes opened, and he could see. He was baptized. He became a Christian.

Jesus had a great work for Saul. He became a missionary. He went everywhere, telling people about Jesus, the Saviour. And he was called Paul.

61
An Earthquake Opens Prison
(*Acts 16:16-40*)

Paul was a great missionary. He went from city to city to preach about Jesus. He went across the great sea. And many people believed on Jesus when they heard Paul.

One day Paul went to a far-away city with his friend Silas. There he preached. And there he helped a little girl who had an evil spirit. He told the evil spirit to leave her. And he made her well.

But the little girl was the slave of some wicked men. They were angry at Paul and Silas. They put Paul and Silas in prison.

The jailor was cruel. He put chains on Paul and Silas. And he put their feet in heavy boards, so that they could not move them.

At night it was dark in the jail. Paul and Silas could not sleep. So they began to sing softly. They sang songs of praise to God. The other prisoners heard them.

Then, suddenly, at midnight, the jail began to shake. It shook so hard that the walls cracked. The chains fell off Paul and Silas. The boards fell off their feet. And the doors of the prison broke open.

The jailor came running to the prison. He saw the doors open. And he thought all the prisoners were gone.

The jailor knew he would be punished if all the prisoners were gone. So he took his sword to kill himself.

But Paul called to him, "We are all here!"

Quickly the jailor brought a light. Then he saw that all the prisoners were there.

He went to Paul and Silas and fell down before them. He said, "Oh, tell me what must I do to be saved?"

Paul said, "Believe on the Lord Jesus Christ." And Paul told him about the Saviour.

That very night the jailor believed, and he was baptized. He took Paul and Silas out of prison. He gave them supper and he washed their sore backs. And in the morning he set them free.

62

A Shipwreck

(*Acts 27*)

Paul was a prisoner again. This time soldiers were going to take him to Rome. The soldiers took him to a big sailboat on the sea. And when a good wind blew, they sailed away.

The boat sailed for many, many days. Then they were far out at sea, and could not see land at all.

And one day the wind began to blow very hard. Big dark clouds covered the sky and hid the sun. The wind blew harder and harder. The waves grew big. And the rain began to fall.

It was a very bad storm. All the men on board the boat were afraid. Even the sailors were afraid.

Day after day the wind blew, the big waves rolled over the boat, and the rain poured down.

But one night an angel came to Paul. The angel said, "Do not be afraid. You must go to Rome, to tell about Jesus there. This boat will go to pieces, but God will save you. And He will save all the other people on the boat."

In the morning Paul talked to the sailors and to all the other people. He said, "Do not be afraid. I know that the ship will go down. But none of us will drown."

Then Paul told them to eat, so that they would be strong. Paul took bread. He looked up to God for a blessing. And he ate. Then the others ate, too.

After a while they saw land. The sailors tried to steer the boat, but they could not. The wind just blew it along to shore. And there the waves broke it in pieces.

But all the people jumped into the water. They all came to land safely.

63

John's Vision

(*Revelation*)

There was a little island called Patmos. On that island, John, the disciple of Jesus, lived alone. Cruel men put him there because he would not stop preaching about Jesus. John was lonely on the island. But he was happy in the Lord.

One Sunday morning John sat alone by the sea. All was very quiet on the island. There was just the lapping of the little waves. And suddenly John heard a voice. The voice was loud, like a horn.

The voice said, "Write in a book the things that you see. And send the book to the churches."

John turned around to see who was talking. And there he saw Jesus!

Jesus was all bright with shining glory. His face was bright as the sun. John was afraid. He fell down on his face.

But Jesus put a hand on John and said, "Do not be afraid. I will show you things that must happen."

Then Jesus showed John many things. He showed the troubles that will come to the earth. He showed how the dead will live again. And He said to John, "I am coming, soon. Everybody shall see me. And all who love me shall come to be with me in heaven, forever."

John wrote all these things in a book. It is the last book of the Bible. Today we are waiting for Jesus to come again. And we shall all see Him.